Guide to Villa d'Este

by
Isabella Barisi

With text by
Dora Catalano, on the decoration of the halls

Consultants
Marcello Fagiolo and Maria Luisa Madonna

DE LUCA EDITORI D'ARTE

Ministero per i Beni e le Attività
Culturali

Soprintendenza per i Beni
Architettonici, per il Paesaggio e per
il Patrimonio Storico Artistico e
Demoetnoantropologico per il Lazio
Via Cavalletti, 2 - 00187 Roma

Soprintendente: Arch. Costantino Centroni

Villa D'este
Piazza Trento, 1
00019 Tivoli (RM)

Director: Arch. Isabella Barisi

Text
Isabella Barisi
Dora Catalano

Consultants
Marcello Fagiolo
Maria Luisa Madonna

Translation by
Bill Rubenstein

Staff
Manlio Benedetti
Pierina De Simone
Simonetta Dominici

Photographs by
Beatrice Pediconi
Gianluca Bianchi
Nico Marziali
(figg. 2, 7, 13, 14, 15, 20, 21, 23, 24, 25, 27,
30, 31, 37, 39, 45, 46, 47, 48, 52, 53, 54, 64,
65, 74, 80, 82, 83, 85, 86, 89, 91, 93, 95, 99,
108, 110, 112, 113, 114)

Superintendency of Photographic Archives
Isabella Barisi (fig. 98)
Manlio Benedetti (figg. 16, 17, 33a, 33b,
34, 69, 78, 84, 106, 107, 111, 115, 116, 117)
Mauro Coen (figg. 36, 49, 50, 73)
Lorenzo De Masi (figg. 18, 105)

Salvatore Giagnoli (figg. 26, 28, 29, 32, 42,
43, 44, 51, 55, 56, 77)

Aerial photos
Aldo Ippoliti – Kamera Studio per Sara
Nistri (figg. 1, 6)

PRESENTATION

Villa d'Este, *"one of the most significant and complete monuments to the culture of the Renaissance, an incomparable example of the Italian Garden..."*
With these phrases, extracted from the complete text, UNESCO has defined its reasons for inscribing the Villa on its list of World Heritage Sites, an honor bestowed in 2001.

"Garden of Marvels," "Garden all'italiana," were among the first and foremost spontaneous expressions used from the beginning – the classic means of describing a villa which has been the model for so many others constructed in Italy and elsewhere.

This, is of course, a status acquired over time – one the splendid complex has earned through the preference revealed by major artists, poets, and musicians from all over the world, who have made it an obligatory point of reference. Even today, this fame beckons thousands of visitors every year. They come – fascinated by the wonders of the original fountains, by the sound of the hydraulic organ, and by the birdsong in the Fountain of the Owl.

The complete ensemble of majestic fountains, grottoes, and nymphaeums is marked by a high classical culture and a profound awareness of allegory and ancient mythological references in large part a tribute to its first patron, Cardinal Ippolito d'Este. The Villa's very concept represents a happy meeting of nature and art – effected by the organic alterations made to the hills to realize the splendid lanes, terraces, paths, and pools, in forms which are sometimes rigidly geometrical and other times more natural in aspect.

Today, everything has been brought back to its ancient splendor through a series of restorations which respect the spirit of the creators – which is to say: classical landscape environments marked with a pronounced romantic spirit. The Garden and the Villa with its magnificent, frescoed public rooms offers to even the most demanding visitors magical emotions and evocative sensations, thanks also to the incomparable setting noted for its sweeping panoramas of the Roman countryside. At present, the monumental complex – property of the Italian State – is under the direct tutelage of the Superintendence and constitutes a cultural asset which offers innumerable resources – including economic ones – as well as being a reference point for the city of Tivoli itself. In its halls are held meetings, conferences, concerts, shows, and other events of great importance which help keep the city a lively place.

Costantino Centroni
Soprintendente
per i Beni Architettonici, per il Paesaggio e
per il Patrimonio Storico-artistico e
Demoetnoantropologico per il Lazio

Statement by which Unesco has inscribed the Villa d'Este in the World Heritage List:

"Villa d'Este at Tivoli, with its palace and garden, is one of the most significant and complete examples of the culture of the Renaissance in its most refined expression. Its innovative concept, the creativity and ingenuity of its architectural works (fountains, basins, etc.) constitutes an incomparable example of the Italian Garden of the 16th century.
Villa d'Este, one of the first "Gardens of Marvels," has always been a model and has had a decisive influence on the development of European gardens.

1. Aerial view of Villa d'Este with the Fishponds and the Fountain of the Organ

INTRODUCTION

Villa d'Este, the masterpiece of the *Giardino all'italiana*, created by Pirro Ligorio for Cardinal Ippolito II d'Este, represented something absolutely new in the panorama of the 16th century villas. Never before – with only the exception of the ancient models – had nature and topography been so massively remodeled to articulate a "hanging garden" with sloping terraces – all giving a titanic impression which stupefied the visitors of its day.

But above all, never before had there been concentrated in one place (only slightly larger than four hectares) such an extraordinary number of fountains, grottoes, and nymphaeums, creating a marvelous environment in which, as Uberto Foglietta wrote to Cardinal Flavio Orsino in 1569, "no matter in which direction one sets one's gaze, there are spouts of varied styles and of such splendor of design that one must conclude that in all the world there could be no such place which is not greatly inferior."

The unlimited hydraulic capacity – guaranteed by the colossal work of channeling the river Aniene – allowed an unprecedented exploration of the dynamic potential of water, experimenting with all possible effects, both visual and acoustic. Water is bent into every imaginable shape – here, multiplying into hundreds of rivulets and spouts for the entire length of a course, there, reversing over a pool like a luminous cylindrical veil.

In one place it shoots out in one single rumbling arc – then, high in the air it is broken into spray. In others it suddenly takes the shape of a lily, an umbrella, a fan, and even giant faces. It can recreate the waterfalls on the Aniene or give the effect of rain, of sunbursts, of boiling water, or a terrifying flood. In still other occasions it is combined with air to create sounds – birdsong, animal cries, bombarde, musket fire, or even the sounds of a trumpet, buccina, and an organ. For the grandiosity of its enterprise, the richness of its decorations, and the extraordinary variety of it waterplays, Villa d"Este became instantly famous in its day and a much copied model in Europe, leading to an apotheosis in the French gardens of Vaux-Le-Vicomte and Versailles.

More than the works and structure of the terracing – conditioned as they were by the unique geography of the site – the innovations of the Villa which had the largest effect on the development on the gardens of the Mannerist and Baroque periods were hydraulic in nature. Here were the first "water theaters," (the great fountains), the first "water ladders," (*scala dei Bollori* and water chains), and the first artificial waterfall (grottoes of the Sibyls).

Villa d'Este – together with Pratolino – is among the first "gardens of marvels," and has exercised an important influence on the successive development of water organs and the culture of "*automi.*" Even during the period in which the Villa was no longer the model to which others referred, it remained in memory a garden of marvels, of delights, of attractions, so much so that its very name – or rather that of its location, Tivoli, became synonymous in the 19th century for a number of amusement parks and private villas.

Even today, at five hundred years of age, Villa d'Este continues to cast its spell, as every year thousands of visitors from every country walk its paths. And, if some of the ancient wonders unfortunately have been lost to time (though they will be nevertheless described in this guide), once again one can listen to the music of the hydraulic organ and the birdsong fountain, both recently brought back to their former glory.

If Villa d'Este owes the durability of its fame to the extraordinary effects produced by a sophisticated utilization of water, one must not forget that with its architectural works (palace, fountains, loggias, nymphaeums, and grottoes) and with its precious decorative elements (such as the pictorial cycles executed by famous artists of the Roman Mannerist School, including Federico Zuccari and Girolamo Muziano), it constitutes one of the most fascinating architectural creations of the Italian Renaissance and is an exceptional synthesis of the values of the period, in which both architectural language and humanistic studies are woven together – as are scientific dedication and a passion for the classical past, hydraulic technology and a complex iconographic program.

2. Water display in the Oval Fountain

IPPOLITO D'ESTE
AND THE CREATION OF THE VILLA

On September 9, 1550, the city of Tivoli celebrated the installation of the new Governor, Ippolito d'Este (Ferrara, 1509-Roma, 1572) with a triumphal welcome "as important to the city as those accorded the Holy Pontiffs," as described by the Tiburtine Chronicler, Giovanni Maria Zappi.

But the long conclave which ended February 8, 1550 elected Julius III (1550-1555). And Ippolito remained the "Pope that never was."

Second son of the Alfonso I, duke of Ferrara and of Lucrezia Borgia, daughter of Pope Alessandro VI, he was therefore the descendent of one of the most illustrious Italian dynasties, the Este, Lords of Ferrara since 1393, whose prestige derived not only from their political role but also from a tradition of liberalism, culture, and patronage of the arts which transformed Ferrara into one of the principle centers of humanism and civilization in Italy in the XVth and XVIIth centuries. From birth, Ippolito was destined to have an ecclesiastical career, and at only ten years of age he was named Archbishop of Milan. Having

3. Ippolito II d'Este (first figure to the right of the candelabra; fresco in the Sala dei Fasti Farnesiani, Palazzo Farnese, Caprarola

completed his humanistic studies, he was sent at 27 to the French court, where he began a relationship of true friendship with the royals and in 1540 he was made a member of the Private Council of Francois I. At 30, Paul III – at the solicitation of the French King – conceded to him the nomination of Cardinal. The protection of Francois I gave Ippolito the possibility of obtaining offices and ecclesiastical advantages that made him the wealthiest Cardinal of his times. His annual income was estimated at 120,000 scudi, an enormous sum which still hardly made up for his vast capability for spending money – indeed all of his life he was besieged by demands from creditors.

He was a munificent protector of an innumerable coterie of artists and literarati who came to his court, among whom we remember only the names of the goldsmith and sculptor Benvenuto Cellini, the musicians Pierluigi da Palestrina and Nicola Vicentino, the Latinists Uberto Foglietta and Marc-Antoine Muret, the architects Sebastiano Serlio and Pirro Ligorio, and the poet Torquatto Tasso. At Rome, where he went in 1549 as representative of Henry II, he immediately became one of the most brilliant characters in the political, artistic, and social life of the city. He chose prestigious residences – competing in some cases even with the Popes themselves; indeed an Ambassador of the Este judged his palace at Monte Giordano "something worthy more of a Pope than a Cardinal." Believing himself predestined to be crowned Pope, he did not hide his ambition and utilized all his economic power to that end, not to mention the political influence and prestige of his family. But as it happened, it was precisely these factors which were to compromise his aspirations in the delicate moment in history that coincided with the beginning of the Council of Trent. And, indeed, fully five times – beginning in 1549 – his hopes were dashed.

During the conclave in which he was presented as the candidate of Henry II of France, just as he managed to increase the number of his backers with astute negotiations and open corruption, there arrived from the house of Hapsburg the Imperial Veto of his nomination. He quickly rescinded his own candidacy and moved to help elect Giovanni Maria del Monte, who, as soon as he was elected, paid him back by ratifying his assignment for life as Governor of Tivoli, which took place in the College of Cardinals December 3, 1549.

The posting was very welcomed by Ippolito as he was a passionate collector of antiquities, and Tivoli thus put a vast archeological patrimony within his jurisdiction.

At this point in history, the wealth of the region still remained essentially unexplored, if already noted in the literature. In all likelihood, even before Ippolito's arrival on the scene, Pirro Ligorio had already begun his studies and reconnaissance on the grounds as official "classicist," a post that he maintained until 1555.

His research covered the field: from excavations in search of statues to the reliefs of the architectural structures and then to the actual facilities of the villas. He started by making a planimetric reconstruction of Villa Adriana and a description of the individual buildings, He also did a geological and morphological analysis of the sites – all covered by commentary, drawings, descriptions, and hypotheses of possible reconstruction – an enormous job, later incorporated into tomes such as "The Books of Antiquity" which were the basis of the planning behind Villa d'Este.

Certainly it was Ligorio who on that first trip saw the potential of the governmental seat to be transformed into "a royal place," as Zappi wrote, and to suggest to Ippolito the idea of realizing on the grounds a fountain garden which

4. Self-portrait of Pirro Ligorio

was to be magnificent and absolutely innovative, even more spectacular than the one which the Cardinal was creating on the Quirinale (the future papal residence).

The Governor's house in Tivoli was the north-east wing of the convent annexed to Santa Maria Maggiore, which, despite the previous works of the governor Bernardino Carvajal and Ercole Gonzaga, were inadequate "for the housing of such a Prince," as observed Antonio del Re, and insufficient for the housing of his significant household. The convent and its complex, however, boasted a magnificent site with a view that took in the entire region, an absolute prerequisite according to the norms of the period for the construction of a palace/villa.

The immediate need was to upgrade the existing structure to the Cardinal's requirements, remodeling the quarters already occupied by the government and annexing the body of the building still used by the Franciscans. But soon the plan was switched to the far grander idea of building a "Tyburtinum" worthy of competing with the Imperial Villa of

5. Villa d'Este in the original plan, etching by Etienne Duperac, 1573

Hadrian himself, visible below on the plain, and with the Villa of Augustus (in reality the Sanctuary of Hercules Victorious) which rose on its imposing terraces near the Porta Romana and which would eventually abut the area destined to become part of the future garden. The site pre-selected was a quarter of the city named the Valle Gaudente, which sloped away steeply from the base of the convent complex, down toward the Via del Colle connecting with the Porta Romana. Despite being inside the medieval city wall, it retained a semi-rural aspect (with a few buildings mixed in with orchards and vineyards and a built up area only on the rise to the north-east towards the Campitelli quarter). Zappi describes the place as "of a rustic and wild character, with small hollows in the ground and also great caverns, which one can say with confidence are filled with wolves and other horrid animals."

The idea of realizing a garden on such a rocky ground, a place both arid and inaccessible, seemed a daunting task, but the unusual steepness of the terrain (a vertical displacement of more than forty-five meters) seemed right for a garden of fountains. To this aim, the builders immediately considered the possibility of harnessing the waters of the river Aniene, the only source deemed able to satisfy the enormous needs of such a venture.

At the end of October, 1550, Cardinal Ippolito acquired various disparate properties in various points of the Valle Gaudente, with which he began to trace out the area of the future garden and in particular defining its maximum width between the apse of S, Pietro and the city wall.

Held up during the following years – first by a diplomatic posting in northern Italy connected to the wars in Parma, then by a mission as "luogotenente" in Siena on the orders of Henry II, he finally returned to Tivoli only in the summer of 1555 with the intention of

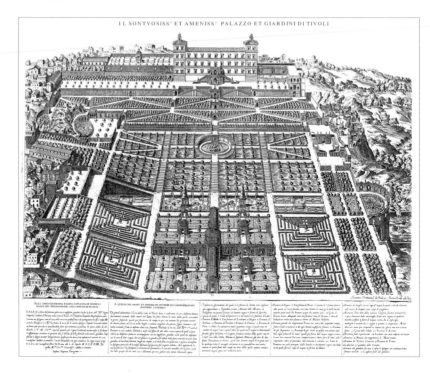

getting down to work on the job of transforming the complex of San Francesco (which is to say, the palace) for which he had set aside considerable sums from as early as the preceding March, and for which he had already obtained from the Franciscans the north-west section of the building in leasehold as of June 10, 1555.

But, shortly thereafter, in September, he was exiled by Paolo IV (1555-1559), under accusation of simony.

In the end it turned out to be Pio IV (1559-1566) who rehabilitated him and reintegrated him in his position as Governor of Tivoli, a title which eventually was modified to the grander: Governor-for-life.

The return to Tivoli in July 1560 thus marked the beginning of construction on the new Villa. The plans were adapted in an etching which Etienne Duperac sent to Catherine de Medici in 1573 and memorialized in the *Descrittione* by an unknown author, which exists in two manuscript versions.

Meanwhile, the area destined to become the garden still lay largely in private hands – and not the Cardinal's. And so, once again began the campaign to acquire land, and, subsequently, to demolish the existing structures. This phase continued until 1569.

To build the garden, the entire balance of the medieval quarter of Campitelli was upset. The old links between various areas of the city were interrupted or disrupted. Citizens were deprived of homes. Public buildings and even ancient religious traditions were sacrificed. Protest, however, was not absent: in 1568 local residents sent to Pio V (1566-1572) a good twelve suits against the Cardinal. The demolition completed, next came the leveling of the terrain.

Both on the hill and towards the Campitelli Quarter terraces were created through the massive movement of rock, as remembered by Zappi in his description of 1576: "The art of the men in the employ of the Cardinal of Ferrara has forced and shattered the nature of the place of the so-called garden with rocks which give a harsh aspect as they are spread around in a frightening manner by men with metal hammers who move them to give shape to what the architects call a garden."

The surplus earth remaining from the earth works was moved to the right side of the garden to enlarge the hanging terraces and to support the artificial terracing using foundations *"al antica"* with pillastered *forti* linked by arcades or barrel vaults, creating vaulted rooms which later were used to make a large number of grottoes, niches, and small nymphaeums.

The works were carried out simultaneously in the various parts of the garden, employing workers for almost three years, from 1563 until May of 1565, during which time the water system was also being worked on. Canals were built starting from the valve under the artificial mountain of the Oval Fountain, where underground pipes more than 200 meters long flowed, this last realized in 1564-65 in order to tap into the waters of the river Aniene.

At the same time, the outlines of the garden began taking form. Based on a grid of perpendicular paths which divided the surface into regular units, or "compartments," it conformed to the aesthetic precepts of the Renaissance, with each module being approximately 30 meters across.

The disposition of the spaces was ordered symmetrically with respect to the longitudinal median axis, which represented the visual reference line of the project, while in the transverse direction, five principal axes constituted the elements of the architectural composition, with systematic creation of lateral visual cones towards the back sides of the fountains, placed to form confined spaces with respect to the context.

The first projects completed, in 1565-1566 labor proceeded on the pictorial decoration of the Palace; in the principal rooms of the lower floor, teams of painters directed by Girolamo Muziano

6. Aerial view of the terraces and foundationsi

and Federico Zuccaari began their work. The work took on a frenetic pace after 1566, when Ippolito, defeated for the fifth time in a conclave and exclude by Pio V from receiving any Papal appointments, turned even more of his energies towards Tivoli.

The Palace complex, now in part already decorated and enlarged towards the south-west on the side facing the garden, was again torn apart by an even larger project. Now that the external work had been, done, the focus turned once again to towards the internal decoration. From 1567-1569 whole teams of painters and stucco artists were set to task – these under the watch of Girolamo Muziano, Livio Agresti, Cesare Nebbia, and Durante Alberti, then Metteo Neroni, who arrived in 1570-1571, and Federico Zuccari, who returned in 1572.

Out in the garden, after the masonry had been completed by Tommaso da Como, he was followed in 1567 by a group of fountain designers (Curzio Maccarone, Luc Leclerc, and Claude Venard), by stone cutters (Raffaello e Biasioto Sangallo) by stucco artists (Paolo Calan-

drino and Luca Figoli) by sculptors (Giovan Battista della Porta, Pirrino del Galgliardo, Gillis van den Vliete, Giovanni Malanca, Pierre de la Motte), as well by mosaicists and ceramicists.

Pirro Ligorio, who returned to the Cardinal's service in 1567-68, directly supervised the work being done on the fountains.

The creation of the villa was conducted according to a scholarly iconographical program, developed by Pirro Ligorio and by humanists in Ippolito's circle. The purpose was to elevate the residence and the Cardinal's person itself, magnifying the sense of his virtue and lineage, and investing the architectural enterprise with dignified significance. Along with the development of symbolic, allegorical, and celebratory themes, all the elements of the composition were planned to create a sense of architectural unity – from the many fountains to the water courses, from the landscaping to the pictorial decoration of the interiors, right through to the installation of ancient statuary. The program, based on a scholarly understand-

7. View of Villa
d'Este around
1568 (fresco in
the Hall of the
Fountain)

ing of the myths and themes of classical culture, was articulated throughout the various areas of the Villa in threads which interwove each artistic discipline and which were comprehensible to the cultivated man of the renaissance, fluent as he was in the symbolism of mythology, even if for us, perhaps, they are less accessible.

After 1569, there was a slowdown in the work, probably due to the weakening of the Cardinal's financial situation, given that he'd already spent a frightening amount of money on the project (on the order of one million scudi or even two!) and that in 1568 he had a reduced income due to the loss of his French assignments. In his later years, Ippolito, who always had suffered from gout, found comfort in spiritual thoughts, in his reading, and in erudite conversations with the intellectuals of his court. Villa d'Este became a temple of culture, a meeting place for the intellectual elite, literati, poets, musicians, etc. In fact, in his funeral oration for the Cardinal, the jurist Ercole Cato described "an academy, a round table, a theater of the world full of singular men, statesmen of every republic."

In the summer of 1572, the work was taken up with a new fever in preparation for the visit of Gregory XIII, which was announced for September 27: a whirlwind of fountain makers, masons, decorators, etchers, and drapers rushed to completion the Fountain of the Dragons and redecorated the rooms of the upper floor. The incredibly sumptuous reception the Pope and his train received cost more than five thousand scudi, pushing even higher the Cardinal's already bulging debts, and forcing him to hock his silver and most precious objects.

The Pope's visit was more than just an extreme homage to one of the most illustrious Cardinals of his time, but also a recognition of his political rehabilitation. But shortly afterwards, on December 2, Ippolito died in Rome, According to his wishes, he was buried in S. Maria Maggiore in Tivoli, beside the villa, where he rests beneath a simple marble slab in front of the high altar, together with his successors, Luigi and Alessandro d'Este.

For centuries, the important collections of sculpture and art objects have been dispersed. Ippolito's residences have been ruined or completely transformed. All that remains bearing witness to his patronage is to be found at Villa d'Este, the home that more than anything else was intended to celebrate the nobility of his lineage and to glorify his virtue.

LATER EVENTS

At the time of Ippolito's death, many fountains were still incomplete and others had not even begun construction. Ippolito's will specified that the Villa would pass to his nephew, Cardinal Luigi (1538- 1586) and that after him it would continue to remain in the pos-. session of the Cardinals of the House of Este, or, in the absence of any, in the possession of the Cardinal Deacon of the Sacred College protempore.

Luigi limited his own efforts to continuing a few works and financing the costly maintainence of what already existed, availing himself of Giovanni Alberto Galvani and, in 1585, of Flaminio Ponzio. In this period, the parade of Cardinals, nobles, and ambassadors – but especially of artists and literati – continued without letup because by now the fame of the Tiburtine retreat was enormous. At this time the Este palace was known as the "Inn of the White Eagle (after the family crest) because it was such a frequent place of lodging for "all the princes, lords, and traveling gentlemen who came to see Tivoli" (A.Del Re). After Luigi's death, the Villa passed to the Cardinal Deacons who left the place

8. "Scene of the Estense Villa in Tivoli" (etching by G.B. Piranesi, 1761

to a slow decay. Only in 1599 was the new Este Cardinal nominated: Alessandro d'Este (1538-1624), who became Governor of Tivoli in 1605, and who began a vast program of works. Gasparo Guerra served as architect. The fountain designers of this phase were Orazio Olivieri, Curzio Donati (from 1611) and Vincenzo Vincenti (from 1619).

Not only were there projects involving maintenance of existing works, and the repair of damage to both vegetation and water systems, but also new projects to build fountains in the lower areas of the garden, not to mention numerous modifications to the garden layout and the fountain decorations.

Alessandro also made a great push to resolve once and for all the issue of ownership and in 1621 received a definitive assignation from Pope Gregorio XV which left the place in the hands of the Este.

Among the Dukes of Modena who followed in succession, Francesco I is worth noting for his numerous restorations between 1629 and 1641 in collaboration with the architect Francesco Peperelli and also for starting a program for transforming the placement of trees in the garden. Cardinal Rinaldo I should also be mentioned, for it was he who commissioned two fountains from Gian Lorenzo Bernini in 1660-1661 and who, in 1670 began an even more extensive campaign of interventions directed by Mattia de Rossi, collaborator of Bernini.

Restorations continued in 1672- 1686 under Duke Francesco II – to whom Giovanni Francesco Venturini dedicated a series of etchings executed in 1685 but published in 1691, which constituted the most complete representation of the garden and its complex of fountains, green areas and the palace.

After 1695 the decline set in, a decay

9. Cardinal Hohenlohe and Liszt in front of the Fountain of the Organ (Salomon Corrodi, Villa d'Este, 1870

which continued for almost two centuries. The Este family could no longer afford to maintain a luxury which they didn't use and which brought in no income.

From 1751 the Palace was stripped of its last furnishings, which were sent to Modena, and the garden and fountains were progressively deprived of their collections of ancient sculptures, which were broken into lots and sold to various buyers across Europe.

The situation got worse after 1796, when, Ercole III was deposed by the French and the property was transferred to the Hapsburg-d'Este. The villa was abandoned and was twice occupied by French troops who devastated the palace and stole even the lead from the fountain conduits.

Between 1850 and 1896, another Cardinal, Gustav von Hohenlohe, acquired the villa *in enfiteusi*, and sought to rescue it from its state of decay, revealing again "in part the comfort and the grandeur which glimmered from its architectural advances, from its vast array of broken and dried up fountains, from its rigorously laid out but now overgrown vegetation, from the still visible

outlines of its flowerbeds." (F.M. Seni). Once again, the villa became a cosmopolitan center of cultural life, frequented by artists, literati, and musicians, among who was Franz Liszt, who visited several times between 1865 and 1885 and, fascinated by the sounds of the waters and by the ancient vegetation, dedicated his pieces *Les jeux d'eau a la Villa d'Este* and *I Cipressi* to the villa.

After the First World War, the property passed to the Italian State. In 1922 the Office of Antiquities and Fine Arts began a vast restoration campaign both of the architecture and the greenery. This lasted more than a decade under the leadership of the honorary conservator Attilio Rossi.

A radically new restoration was executed in the second postwar period – this to repair bomb damage suffered in 1944. Due to particularly bad environmental damage which led to rapid and severe degradation of the walls, these labors were ultimately prolonged and continue even today under the care of the Superintendence of Architectural Assets and for the Landscape and for the Art Historical Patrimony and Demo-ethno-anthropology of Lazio.

THE HYDRAULIC MACHINE

To feed the 51 fountains and nymphaeums, with 398 spouts, 364 jets, 64 waterfalls, 220 basins (of various shapes and sizes), and 875 linear meters of water chains and canals, the entire garden is laced with an intricate network of tunnels, canals, and underground tubes which comprise a highly refined and complex "hyrdaulic machine" which moves exclusively due to the force of gravity.

The idea was suggested to Pirro Ligorio by the extraordinary formation of the Tiburtine soil which was famous even in ancient times for the exceptional abundance of water: beyond the principal branch of the River Aniene which revealed itself in a spectacular waterfall beneath the acropolis, secondary streams ran like vessels un-

derground, with collectors, tunnels, and tubes which provisioned the buildings and public fountains, and which broke out later in picturesque little cascades all along the fronts of the marble platform on which the city was constructed.

It was in fact the idea of returning to this tradition that was behind the project of bringing the waters of the Aniene to feed Villa d'Este, imagined as it was like an artificial mountain perforated by multiple underground veins, analogous to the hills of Tivoli. The hydraulic facility, based on an understanding of ancient Roman technology illustrated in the works of Vitruvius and Frontino, constituted in its whole a masterpiece of hydraulic engineering, not only for the many and

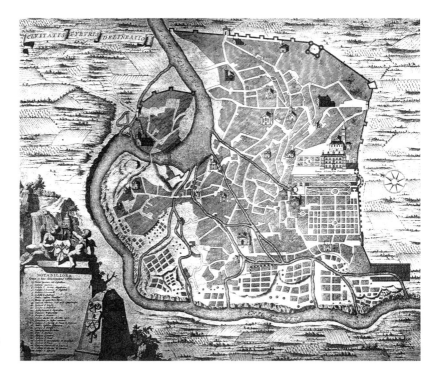

10. Map of Tivoli with the underground canals (Daniel Stoopendal, 17th C.)

fantastic water plays, but also for the general plan by which its water was delivered and distributed.

The scheme was planned in such a way so that the waters which drained from one fountain would then feed into the intakes of fountains on a lower level in the garden, thus greatly reducing the total water needs of the complex and a simplification of the entire system. The first operation for bringing in water (beginning in 1560-1561) involved the Rivellese aqueduct which fed the public fountains situated in the square across from Santa Maria Maggiore, from where the flow was broken into three channels. The first entered the courtyard of the palace and served the Fountain of Venus. The outflow from this fountain was used to fill the reservoir beneath the courtyard (which also served as a cistern collecting rainwater which fell on the palace roof); from this cistern, tubes fed the fountain known as Manica Lunga, (Long Sleeve), the rustic fountain of the lower floor salon, and the fountains of the upper level of the garden (Leda, Pandora, the Tripod, and then the Bicchierone).

The second channel fed a large reservoir positioned underground in the piazza of Santa Maria Maggiore and which, in turn provided flow into several fountains in the Secret Garden and another reservoir still at a lower level (built into the foundations of an ancient Roman villa). From this last reservoir the water flowed into the Fountain of Europa, the Fountain of Pegasus, and into the upper part of the Oval Fountain (through cascades in the rocks and water plays into the semi-oval gallery).

The third channel ran directly into the a small reservoir which served the Fountain of the Unicorn in the Secret Garden.

The flow of the Rivellese aqueduct was modest (maximum 5 litres/second) and therefore the various cisterns, which provided a total of 1000 cubic metric of storage, were indispensable for the various requirements of the complex. The fountains served by the Rivellese, obviously, therefore, could only function for limited periods of time.

In 1564-65, a more substantial conduit was built, following the paths of several ancient Roman canals, to connect up the complex with the waters of the river Aniene slightly above the celebrated waterfalls, thus providing an unlimited flow – now determined to be 500 litres/second.

The waters from the Aniene entered the villa just above the Oval Fountain, where two chambers distributed them to their various destinations, and, if necessary, to the channels leading out of the garden.

A first fork furnished water to the

11. Tivoli – The Cascades (Philippe Benoist, lithography in color, 19th C)

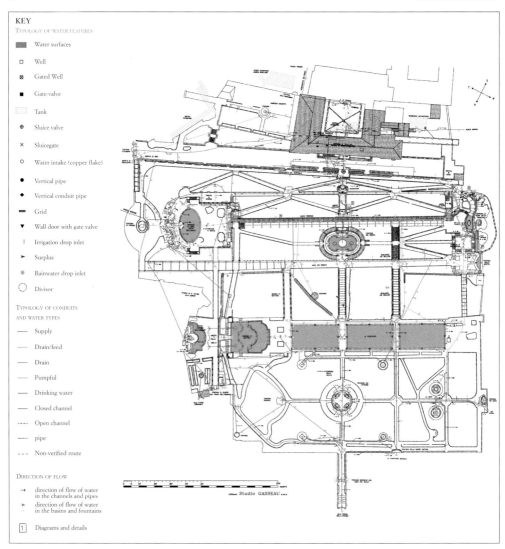

KEY

TYPOLOGY OF WATER FEATURES

▬   Water surfaces

☐   Well

⊠   Gated Well

■   Gate-valve

▭   Tank

⊕   Sluice valve

✕   Sluicegate

○   Water intake (copper flake)

●   Vertical pipe

◆   Vertical conduit pipe

▭   Grid

▼   Wall door with gate valve

I   Irrigation drop inlet

➤   Surplus

⊛   Rainwater drop inlet

◌   Divisor

TYPOLOGY OF CONDUITS
AND WATER TYPES

───   Supply

───   Drain/feed

───   Drain

───   Pumpful

───   Drinking water

───   Closed channel

----   Open channel

---   pipe

- - -   Non-verified route

DIRECTION OF FLOW

→   direction of flow of water
    in the channels and pipes

➤   direction of flow of water
    in the basins and fountains

1   Diagrams and details

Studio GASSEAU s.a.s.

12. The
Hydraulic
Installations of
Villa d'Este
(relief by
Leonardo
Lombardi;
drawing by
Studio Gasseau)

large canal running longitudinally which fed the Hundred Fountains, the Dragons, the Rometta, Proserpina, the Owl, and practically all the other fountains, including *the Scalinetta dei Bollori, le Mete*, and the other water chains bordering the stairs descending to the Garden level.

Another fork fed an underground canal which passed under the church of San Pietro, reaching the *castellus*

acque of the Organ Fountain, then entering a second tunnel which fed the cascade under the Organ Fountain. From the terrace of the Organ Fountain, the waters reached the fountains on the north side of the garden and the fishponds, from where they collected in one of three outlets which even today provide irrigation water for agricultural and industrial use outside the city of Tivoli proper.

The contemporary facility maintains the general distribution and operation plan of the 16th century waterworks executed by Tomasso Ghinucci, even if there has been a progressive replacement of materials.

At the end of the 19th century, the Rivellese acquduct, by now worn out, was replaced with the "Acqua Marcia" which offered so little water to the villa that even the occasional use of all the fountains of the Secret Garden and the upper garden was no longer possible. When in 1930, the villa was opened to the public, it became necessary to address this lack by adding a new source of water to the system. Again the Aniene was called upon, the waters of which were pumped up from the intake valve on the Mountain of the Oval Fountain to the cistern beneath the palace courtyard, from whence it was distributed via the original system.

The enormous amount of water utilized then and now by the complex, on the one hand represents the most characteristic and attractive element of the Este complex; on the other hand, it is the project's weakest link because the continuous spraying naturally degrades the mechanisms, which are constantly soaked by nebulized water, which progressively degrades the surfaces and materials. The conservation problems are aggravated by the poor chemical quality of the water itself, which, coming as it does from a river, is heavily laden with sediment (including seeds) and silt, especially during rainy periods. Considerable masses of slimy substances are constantly being deposited not only in the basins but also on the decorative surfaces of the fountains and on the modeling of the sculptural groups which are quickly covered over with a thick layer of vegetation of weeds. Lately, the situation has worsened with the formation of

lime deposits due to the hardness of the water from the river, which covers the surfaces and blocks up the canals, tubes, and jets. The management of the complex has therefore always been a difficult job because even just to keep the water flowing requires constant maintenance. For this reason please don't be too upset if, during your visit you happen to find a fountain or two inoperative!

In the last years, however, the biochemical quality of the water has noticeably improved with the installation of water purifying equipment by the government of the Lazio Region during the years 1999-2000. This equipment, technologically in the avantgarde, guarantees a partial decalcification, filtering of some silt and sediment, and anti-bacterial treatment with UV lamps before the intake at the Este canal.

13. Play of water in the Fountain of Neptune

THE PALACE
AND THE DECORATIVE SCHEME

Today one enters the villa only via the door adjacent to the church of San Francesco (or Santa Maria Maggiore) which originally comprised the entrance reserved for Cardinal Ippolito d'Este and his court. The complex was conceived to be seen from below, from the entrance on the ancient via Tiburtina, now via del Colle, from which point one began the slow route upward, thus slowly discovering the aquatic "marvels" of the garden, passing through the ever unfurling visual pageant of the terraces culminating finally up at the Palace.

Ippolito's lack of interest in the entrance on Piazza Trento is indicated by the door, which remains the same as in the times of Bernardino Carvajal, governor of Tivoli until 1521, as is indicated on the crest of the arch and the inscription above. Cardinal d'Este is remembered by the large oval crest in travertine, installed on the doorway at the beginning of the 20th century.

From the piazza, beyond the high boundary wall, one can see the lateral facade of the palace which corresponds to the north-east wing of the convent of S. Francesco (or S. Maria Maggiore), then used as residence by the governors of Tivoli.

The convent itself was built by the Benedictines in the 9th century on the remains of a Roman villa and was later enlarged and modified by the Franciscans, who obtained it in 1256 from Pope Alessandro IV.

The structure of the convent occupied an area essentially corresponding to the contemporary palace, except for the lateral enlargement, and was already three stories in height, as is illustrated by the wall design of the lateral façade in stone blocks, traceable to the 13th century, with windows and slits between the 16th century openings.

Passing through the entrance, the first room of the palace is a **Foyer** (n. **1**) "comfortably wide and spacious," (Del Re, 1611) adorned with a rounded vault once covered with paintings. These appear ruined today, a result of the bombing in 1944 and now stitched together by obvious repairs. The pictorial decoration of the walls suggests a simulation of ancient marble; the vault develops an articulated architectural grid, enlivened by the presence of birds in flight, scallop shells, and grotesque motifs.

In the figurative panels, there are monochrome illustrations from the Old Testament, unfortunately either badly damaged or totally lost. One can still make out, however, the *Great*

14. The church of S. Maria Maggiore and the entrance door to Villa d'Este

Flood, Cain and Abel, some episodes of the *Life of Moses, of Jacob, and David*. The best preserved scene illustrates the *Sacrifice of Isaac*. The paintings are ascribed to a first phase of work around 1563-1565 under the direction of Girolamo Muziano, probably by artists from Emilia. Attached to the foyer one finds two rooms today used to welcome visitors. The bombardments of the last war destroyed the frieze depicting ancient mythological themes which ran along the walls of the reception room. In the following **Hall of the Stories of Solomon,** (n. **2**) today used as the tick-

15. on the preceding page: View of the garden from the lower entrance on via del Colle

16. Detail of the frieze in the Hall of the Stories of Solomon

et office, some pictures which had been removed after the war damage were recently returned to their original positions. The frieze, today not wholly legible, was dedicated to the Stories of Solomon, from his proclamation as King of Israel to the holy prophecy of the division of the Kingdom. The stories were done in monochrome and inserted inside a fake marble frame, with the crests of the Cardinals placed in the corners under a sort of fabric canopy. The scenes, thus placed in the front of the composition, seemed inserted into

the "Michelangelesque" culture which characterized much Roman painting after the middle of the 16th century. Like the pictures of the foyer, they were probably executed by 1565 by more artists under Muziano's direction.

Leaving the ticket office, before entering the courtyard one finds on the left a niche containing a Colossal Head in travertine from the 16th century. It is placed on a pedestal on which were assembled majolica pieces in a 16th century attempt at restoration. This sculpture and its twin, located in the niche

17. Theporticoed courtyard of the Palace

beyond the courtyard, were transferred here in 1765 from the garden, where they had been kept "in a hidden place," as indicated in archival documents. From the foyer one passes into the porticoed **courtyard**, (n. **3**) realized in the area where previously there had been the convent cloister, of which only a few architectural elements remain, such as the mullioned window on the south west wall.

Done in rounded arches set on travertine pilasters, it was executed by Raffaello Sangallo in 1566-1567 and developed on three sides, thus masking the anomalies of the facility. The planimetric conformation of the palace, in fact, reveals notable irregularities based on the pre-existing conditions, since the body of the building to the northeast, corresponding to the old government building was oblique with respect to the wing of the convent facing the valley, of which one can still make out the masonry texture – even in the original left visible, on the north-west wall of the courtyard above the portico. In the courtyard, beside the church of S. Maria Maggiore, the **Fountain of Venus** (n. **4**) is the only such fixture of the villa which conserves intact the original sculptural fittings.

The architectural make-up is in bossed travertine, with a system of triumphal arches with only one "*fornice*" framed by pairs of Doric columns. It is the work of Raffaello Sangallo (1568-69). Above the cornice is found the 4th century A.d. bust of the Emperor *Constantine* in marble. It rests on a base decorated with a large mask, both pieces the work of the 16th century. In the small niche, is the Roman (2nd-3rd century A.d.) statue of Venus "who sleeps to the murmur of water" (Foglietta), leaning on a vase, only partially conserved, which originally sprayed water into the basin beneath, a Roman *labrum* in white marble, with two curried bands decorated with two lion heads (2nd century A.d.).

The base of the niche is decorated with a precious bas-relief in stucco, the work of Curzio Maccarone (perfectly conserved, even if it has lost part of the original gilding). This represents the course of the Rivellese from its source on Mt. Sant'Angelo to the villa, passing along the way a landscape of rocks, windmills, bridges, and rural edifices. Along the arcade one finds branches of quince trees – these allude to the 11th labor of Hercules, the theft of the golden apples from the garden of the Hesperides, where they had been guarded by the dragon Ladone.

This is the first representation from the myth of Hercules – the most frequently found symbolic source in the Este garden, explicitly declared in the epigram of Marc-Antoine Muret: "The golden apples which Hercules stole from the sleeping Dragon / now Ippolito possesses/ grateful of the gift, he wishes on its author/ that the gardens he has planted – to him be dedicated."

18. The Fountain of Venus in the courtyard

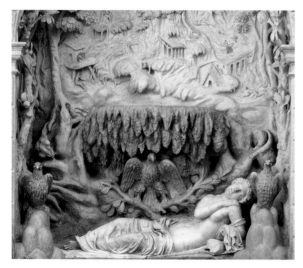

19. The Venuses
Nimpha Loci
between Este
Eagles in the
Fountain of
Venus

Cardinal Ippolito; others were brought later.

In the *oculi* purposely carved into the masonry corresponding to the access to the apartments, there are fake marble decorations; originally there were classical marbles here. Today one sees three unrelated sculptures, among which is the Germanic Head, just barely sketched out, which Pacifici (1925-23) dates to the XI- XIIth centuries.

By tradition, the sarcophagus positioned beneath the mullioned window in the portico to the south-west was brought here by Cardinal Ippolito d'Este from the nearby church of S. Pietro to use as a basin under a fountain. It is clearly late medieval work from roman marble and certainly must have once been finished with mosaic tiles. The support bases, on the other hand, are dateable to the XVIth century. The other objects beneath the loggia were brought to the villa at the beginning of the 20th century. Worthy of mention among them is the sarcophagus with banded body, placed along the north-west wall, dated to the 3rd or 4th century A.D. and perhaps a discovery from excavations in the territory of Cineto Romano.

Above the sarcophagus, a travertine plaque recalls the frequent visits here of Franz Liszt, who stayed in a small apartment on the top floor where he composed and played the piano in a delightful round studio called the "Room of the Rose." This is now used by the management for offices and may be visited only by scholars by appointment. From the courtyard, passing the great glass door and the landing of the stairs, one enters the **Corner Hall** (n. **5**) now used as a screening room for a film about the villa (showings in four languages in continuous rotation, film length about 30 minutes). The large space was originally covered in leather vestments and was never decorated with paintings, except in the recesses of the windows.

The ceiling *a lucunari* in plaster paint-

Hercules, central figure of the iconological program, is twice tied to the villa: he is one of the divine protectors of the Tiburtine region and the legendary founder of the house of Este. By analogy, the villa is thus a celebration also of the labors of Ippolito, who as in the antecedent myth has also faced memorable "labors" to create his garden and so can thus exhibit the golden apples as a kind of personal emblem—now protected by the Este Eagle.

The fountain anticipates other themes that we will see again in the decoration of the palace and garden: the celebration of nature and the beauty of the Tiburtine soil, the theme of the life enhancing water which here makes it entrance in the villa, and Venus, depicted as the *Nympha loci*, protectress of the springs, taking up a much noted iconographical motif of the 16th century, derived from the fountain in Rome by Angelo Colocci.

Left of the fountain is placed a titanium plate which commemorates the inclusion of Villa d'Este on the World Heritage List.

In the courtyard we find a group of stone objects: sculptures, sarcophaguses, and architectural elements. Some of these were gathered here by

ed to simulate timber is the product of a restoration done to repair war damage. From the Corner Room, one enters, on the right, **the Hall of Landscapes with Hunting Scenes** (n. **6**) which today houses multimedia displays available for use by the public. Before 1944, a frescoed frieze ran along the wall; today the only surviving part can be found on the wall towards the courtyard.

These pictures had previously been attributed to Antonio Tempesta, a Florentine who specialized in landscapes; today scholars tend to lean instead towards Flemish masters and date the work to the 1580s. This puts the work into the most fecund phase of the vogue of the hunting picture. The surviving scenes depict important personages in rustic clothes, accompanied by their weapons, during a hunt for ducks and heron. One of the scenes appears to be set in a landscape suggesting the Tiber near the Tiburina island. Returning towards the Corner Room, one can now move towards the two rooms positioned along the principle prospect. In Ippolito's time both were covered in yellow satin. Today they conserve at least the pretty ceilings lined with 16th century *lacunari*. In the hollow of a window of the first room, there is a fresco depicting the Tiburtine countryside with the church of S. Maria di Quintiliolo, the same image the visitor can see looking out the window.

The **Second Room** (n. **7**) is dedicated to the exhibition of a small nucleus of easel paintings by the Roumenian artist Virginia Tomescu Scrocco, these donated by her heirs. The artist, born in Bucarest in 1886, completed her training in Paris and Roma, moving to Tivoli around 1915 together with her husband, the Doctor Amadeo Scrocco, and quickly transformed her house into a meeting place for artists and intellectuals of the region. All of the works displayed are either depictions of Tiburtine landscapes or of noted persons in the cultural life of the city.

Leaving now the last room connected to the Cardinal's family, one enters his personal residence, starting with the **Salon** (n. **8**).

This large space, placed centrally in the building, was used for receptions. In the 16th century, the walls, now bare, were covered with leather printed with gold and green with edges of eagles, known about today because of a payment of 150 scudi to the *orpellaio* Michele di Domenico. Among the furniture was once found a table used to play "trucco," a sort of renaissance billiards. The table, like those of today, was covered with green cloth.

The upper part of the room was covered with frescoes, with the frieze of *Virtù* along the walls and grotesques on the pavilion vault, separated by stucco framing. The pictorial organization of the room is from 1568 and was done by a vast team of artists directed by the painter Livio Agresti, called specifically by Ippolito because he had seen oth-

20. Vault of the studio of Liszt, known as "Room of the Roses"

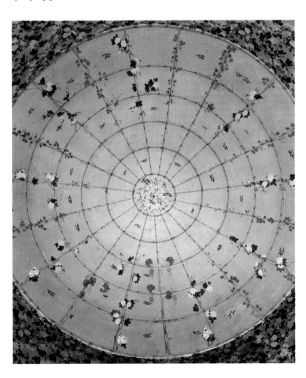

21. The Salon of
the Upper Floor

22. Allegorical
figures of *Virtù*
in the frieze of
the Upper Floor

23. View with
*Tiburtine
Landscape* on the
ceiling of the
Upper Salon

24. View of the
Garden from the
Upper Salon

25. Coat-of-arms of Cardinal Ippolito on the ceiling of the Ante-chamber

26. Detail of the grotesques on the ceiling of the Ante-chamber

er work already in Este possession in Emilia.

Stucco workers including Tivolino also participated, as did masters from Tuscany, Lombardy, and the Marches, not to mention Flemish artists, almost certainly responsible for the beautiful landscapes.

Along the frieze one can see twenty personifications of *Virtu* (each with an inscription) alternating with undecorated oval frames. These, like the large empty squares on the vault, were meant to sport "pictures of worthy men" which were never realized, due to the Cardinal's death. The complex decorative system of the vault is an informed

mix of multiple elements: the curious, humanized *telemoni*, the deformed faces of fauns, the humorous winged genii, the allegory of the Four Seasons, the river Gods, the festoons of fruit and vegetables. Throughout one finds the lily, the eagle, and the apple, motifs from the Cardinal's personal emblem. On the larger sides Landscapes are much in evidence, all freely inspired from the Tiburtine site: one can recognize the ruined temples, such as the Sibilla, placed on the side of the streams and waterfalls.

Leaving the loggia, one enjoys a first view of the garden and the Tiburtine panorama.

As described by Zappi (1576): "one sees the entire city, with the garden, the wild olives, the mountains rising around the city, the great plain and countryside, not only that of Rome but all the way to Ostia, which is thirty miles (…) one sees and discovers all the gardens with the river Aniene and even sees the villa of Quntilio Varo, and the Villa of Emperor Hadrian, and simultaneously the villa of Emperor Octavian, it is said to be one of the most beautiful views in the world and above this, if the morning be fair and clear, one sees the city of Rome and the outline of St. Peter's."

The floor is terra cotta and contains bands including late 19th century and modern majolicas which recreate the original 16th century models.

Continuing, one passes the so-called "Camerone" or "**Antechamber**" (n. **9**). Here, too, the frieze and vault are ascribed to Livio Agresti in collaboration with the same able group of stuccoers and painters. In the frieze one discovers the sixteen *Virtus*, standing portraits alternating with stucco frames. On the vault, capricious grotesques frame little slices of nature and the elaborate frames lead the eye to the crowning panel, boasting the Cardinal's coat of arms supported by two angels. Now we pass into the **Cardinal's Bedroom**, (n. **10**) which we must try to

27. Wooden ceiling *a cassetoni* in the bedroom of Ippolito II d'Este

imagine with its walls covered with precious leather painted with gold and silver, executed in 1567 by the Florentine craftsman Michele de Domenico, maker of the printed leather wall coverings in the Salon. The coffered wooden ceiling is notable. It is a precious artifact which fortunately has survived the years in excellent condition right down to its pictorial ornamentation. Work began on it in 1569 by the master carver Giovanni da Tivoli, and it was painted and gilded with gold leaf by a "Leandro Romanesco" and a "Battista Veneziani," otherwise unknown. The central compartments, the Este Crest crowned by a Cardinal's hat is flanked by the cardinal's personal emblem, the eagle surrounded by quince branches and accompanied by the motto *"ab insomnia non custodita dracone."* The motto, taken from a verse by Ovid,

28. Figure of an orchard keeper in the Hall of Arts and Crafts

29. Allegorical figure of *Tibur* in the Hall of Arts and Crafts

30. on the following page: Chapel

refers to the 11th labour of of Hercules, the taking of the golden apples of the Hesperides.

The frieze below offers another theory on the allegory of Virtu, realized under the same commission as that in the preceding rooms by Livio Agresti's team. The feminine figures, identified by inscriptions and by various attributes, are seated in pairs on the sides of the oval stucco cornices. Compared with the previous rooms, the pictures have more vivid, even brash, colors and assume a greater ornamental effect. The following room, the **Hall of Arts and Trades**, (n. 11) was also part of the Cardinal's personal residence. The frieze which lends the room its present name is the result of work done in 1924, promoted by the Honorary Conservator of the villa, Attilio Rossi. Among those called upon to realize the powerful figures of craftsmen and laborers, (symbols of various trades) which surround the allegorical figure of Tibur, was Emilio Notte (1891-1982). He took inspiration from the 16th century friezes in the other rooms, transforming them into the language of

symbolism, influenced by his relationship with friends who were part of the Roman Secession. Local tradition identifies the portraits as craftsmen and farmers of Tivoli. We know now, however, that the various faces of the townsfolk actually were from nearby Castel Madama, birthplace and residence of Atillio Rossi.

From this room, one passes into the **Gallery** (n. 12) , the only room on the upper floor to conserve its original terra cotta floor. In Ippolito's time, this space was also covered with leather painted with gold and silver, glazed red with black borders.

At the end of the Cardinal's apartment, one finds the small **Chapel** (n. 13), the work of Federico Zuccari who, with various assistants, completed it in the spring of 1572.

Here, Zuccari has attempted a solution previously used for the circular chapel in Palazzo Farnese in Caprarola, where the walls were transformed by an elaborate architecture illusion to make a background for the imposing figures of *Prophets and Sibyls.* The flattened ionic decorative pilasters subdivide the space into bas-relief compartments in monochrome with episodes relating to various personages. The *Prophets and Sibyls,* which dominate the narrow space, emerge powerfully from the compartments, certainly representing one of the most important pictorial groups of the palace. Their quality and stylistic details surely indicate here the hand of Zuccari.

Zuccari's assistants, on the other hand, must have worked on the pictures on the barrel vault, where, inside the elegant frames in gilded stucco is the cycle of the exaltation of the Virgin, culminating with the *Coronation* in the center. The scenes depict different episodes in the life of Mary: the *Birth of the Virgin*, the *Marriage with Joseph*, the *Visitation*, the *Presentation of Jesus at the Temple*, and finally, the *Death of the Virgin*. On the altar, one can see a fresco depicting the noted Madonna

della Ghiara, a copy of a painting done in the church of the same name in Reggio Emilia by the painter Giovanni Bianchi in 1573, based on a drawing by Lelio Orsi.

Returning to the Hall of Arts and Trades, one reaches the courtyard crossing the long gallery which links the courts with the Great Loggia (corresponding to the "long sleeve" of the lower floor.) Across the courtyard one reaches the **Public Staircase** (n. **14**) which leads to the lower floor. The two niches on the entrance landing and the two analogues on the junction point between the ramps house various unrelated statues, such as the headless Venus in peperino, which was probably found in the garden.

On the lower floor, one finds, on the left, the **Corridor of the Long Sleeve** (n. **15**) which leads to various rooms. Certainly inspired from ancient *criptoportici* (one thinks of the one at Villa Adriana) both in its use of a barrel vault, and in the system of illumination using sky lights punched through the ceiling to the courtyard above.

31. *Sybil* and *Prophets* (frescoes in the Chapel)

32. *Coronation of the Virgin* (fresco on the ceiling of the Chapel)

33a and 33b: Rustic Fountains in the "Manica Lunga"

34. Detail of the mosaic on the ceiling of the "Manica Lunga"

35. "Manica Lunga"

The long walkway consented "healthy and welcome strolls from the internal rooms" (U. Foglietta); in the last section, where the windows face towards the Courtyard of the Pallacorda, it permitted guests and courtiers to watch the games out of the summer sun.

The first section of the "long sleeve" was decorated with frescoes in 1565, and shortly thereafter redone with the present mosaics in a rustic style designed to simulate a **flowery pergola** inhabited by birds, inspired by pergolas typical of 16th century villa gardens. The decoration reveals some technical discontinuities due to successive restorations – the oldest parts have a denser and more sophisticated mosaic texture and are marked by the use of precious marble (ancient yellow for the flower petals, porphyry green for the leaves), as well as the more naturalistic representation of the birds (one notes the multicolored images of the rooster). Along the *criptoportico*, in correspondence with the openings towards the room, one finds **three rustic fountains** (n. **16**).

The second and the third are the work of Ludovico De Negri and of "Andrea Fontaniere" in 1569. Elegant and cultivated in architecture, they owe their exquisite aura to the colorful mosaic adornments of precious materials which illustrate various geometrical shapes or floral motifs. After 1571, the third fountain was installed (the first coming from the stairs). It is less sophisticated in workmanship and distinguished by the stucco caryatids. To enjoy the complete tour of the complex – and to respect the figurative program intended by the Cardinal, it would be appropriate now to return back to the travertine door visible in back at the base of the stairs.

Here one enters the **Hall of Noah** (n. **17**), placed at the north-east corner of the palace and linked to the Secret Garden. Even at first approach, one notes the different atmosphere of this environment compared to that on the upper floor, not to mention the different character of the decorative figures. In fact, the entire decoration of the lower floor has a less official tone and develops iconographical themes connected to nature, mythology, and water. These spaces hosted the most "private" moments in the life of the Cardinal: the convivial hours, the time of music and poetry, of religious reflection, and the expression of culture. In the Room of Noah, the walls are frescoed to simulate great tapestries bor-

36. *The Sacrifice of Noah* (fresco on the ceiling of the Hall of Noah)

dered with fringes, arranged like drapes on the false travertine of the doors.

Inside, they reveal fantastic scenes, with trees whose trunks spring up like scenery. Ancient buildings, ruins, rustic farm houses on the edge of mirrored pools are set in a measured progression of planes which lead the eye to the horizon, where the colors of water blends into that of the sky. Between dark rain clouds and the light of a colorful dawn, birds take flight.

Recent studies ascribe these works –and the decorative planning of the entire room – to Girolamo Muziano – already famous in his day for his landscapes in the Venetian style. It is likely that, being engaged in the Roman residence of the Cardinal, he entrusted the actual execution of the walls to the landscape specialist, Mattero Neroni, and the ceiling to a group of artists coordinated by a young Tuscan painter, Durante Alberti. The figures have been dated to 1571, that is to the last phase of the decorative campaign of the palace.

On the vault, the bizarre grotesques frame the personages of the *Four Seasons* and the two allegories of *Prudence* and *Temperance*. The corner joins, rimmed by female *ermes*, house the coat-of-arms of Ippolito. In the central frame, Noah himself is depicted, shortly after the flood – with the ark on the summit of Mt. Ararat – as he makes his agreement with God. The subtext is that of the divine will that dominates water, with an implicit reference to the works of the Cardinal here at the villa. This also explains the relief given to the white eagle, alluding to the emblem of Ippolito, placed in the foreground between the animals leaving the ark.

One is tempted to read an analogus symbolic valence also in the adjacent **Hall of Moses** (n. **18**). In the central frame of the vault, Moses, striking the rock with his rod, brings forth the water to quench the thirst of the people of Israel in their flight from Egypt.

37. Moses brings forth the waters (ceiling fresco in the Hall of Moses)

This is an allusion to the Este, who almost miraculously have brought water to the villa, conveying it through conduits carved into the rock. The Room of Moses was decorated, like the preceeding room, by Durante Alberti, almost certainly under the supervision of the ever-present Muziano. The ceiling is divided by multicolored ornamental bands, with grotesques filling the large light fields. There is also – in an almost unique instance en the house – the hydra with seven heads – emblem of Ercole I d'Este, ancestor of Ippolito. Along the walls, a false loggia leads to fantastic painted landscapes, framed by *ermes*, similar to those in the Room of Noah. Both on the two real doors and also on the illusionary (painted) ones, there are panels illustrating the *Stories of Moses*, starting with his discovery on the banks of the Nile.

Next is the **Hall of Venus** (n. **19**). In the old days, even before entering, the visitor could hear the sound of water running along the rocks of the artificial cliff realized inside a grotto framed by an architectural elevation in stucco. In the center was "a statue of a woman in white marble, in a supine position, with her face and anterior parts turned towards the sky, asleep… and a little deer, who is emerging from some caverns in the fountain" (Del Re, 1611). Venturini's etchings (1685) reveal, on

the sides, two female figures pouring water from an amphora into a square basin. The present appearance of the work has been modified. The basin has been eliminated and the original sculptures replaced with gesso statues of *Peace* and *Religion*, a 19th century work commissioned by Gustav von Hohenlohe. These, part of a process of "Christianization" of the decorative scheme of the villa, were an attempt to transform the grotto from one dedicated to Venus (already absent) to one serving instead the cult of the *Madonna of Lourdes*. The room is otherwise bare of decoration with the exception of the beautiful painting on canvas found on the ceiling, 17th century work of delicate classicism, depicting a languid *Venus*, being offered flowers by several angels.

The flooring here is worth noting. It is original, in terra cotta, with the motif of the Este eagle; and can be seen both in this room and in the one before. Returning to the Room of Noah we now continue the tour, visiting the rooms along the principle prospect of the palace.

Now we enter the **Second Tiburtine Hall** (n. **20**) which should be studied together with the **First Tiburtine Hall** (n. **21**). The decorations in both rooms are linked thematically, as well as by their workmanship. Their realization was the fruit of a team of painters led by Cesare Nebbia before 1569. Despite the overall unity of effect, it is possible to recognize the hands of several artists (documentary sources cite several well known by scholars: Matteo de Lecce, Palma the Younger, Gaspare Gasparini).

The decoration of both rooms is characterized by a well defined architectural system. The perimeter is circumscribed by a base vested in marble on which are placed columns. The overall symmetry is achieved with a tasteful use of fake doors painted to simulate the real ones. Flower paintings fill the empty spaces between columns and frame

FONTANA DI VENERE IN VNA DELLE CAMMERE VLTIME DEL PALAZZO
Gio. Giacomo de Rossi le Stampa in Roma alla Pace con Priu: del S. Pont   Gio. Francesco Venturini del. et fc. 6

40. Ceiling of the Second Tiburtine Hall (in the central frame, the *Triumph of Apollo*, and lower, *Sybil*, and *The Aniene*. Higher: the personifications of the *Three Tiburtine Rivers*)

41. *Venus amidst sea foam* (fresco in the Second Tiburtine Room)

the fake tapestries with their narrative scenes, all done in the style of Mannerism. The vaults themselves are also utilized almost as decorative bands. Monochrome medals, masks, and inventions of every kind appear, with the addition, in the First Room, of angels who sport the crest of the Cardinal. Among other things, one also finds the pictures of the *Four Seasons* (First Hall) and the *Muses* (Second Hall).

The themes depicted in the two rooms are connected to the legendary stories of the site. In the room where we are standing the narrative line revolves around the *Tiburtine Sibyl*.

According to the myth of Apollodoro, Queen Ina was punished by Jupiter for having raised young Bacchus. In order to escape the fury of her husband Atamante, Venus and Nepture trans-

formed her into Leucotea. Arriving in Italy together with her younger son Portumno, she took on the name Sybilla Albunea, or more commonly, the *Tiburtine Sibyl.*

Leucotea was hidden near a spring in the Tiburtine Forest – where she prophesized the future and made other oracular pronouncements.

The story of the Sibyl is linked with another myth of the site: the story of the King Annius, who, pursued Mercury – kidnapper of his daughter Cloris – and in so doing, drowned in the river that took on his name.

On the ceiling of this room, both myths are illustrated: The Madness of Atamante, who murders his son Clearco (in back we observe Ino making her escape); and The Death of Annius, on horseback, being swept down by the waters in the vain attempt to reach Mercury.

In the center of the vault is the Triumph of Apollo, dressed as the sun, depicted riding on his *quadriga*, In the pictures on the long sides of the ceiling we see on one side the personification of *Three Tiburtine Rivers* (Tiber, Aniene, Erculaneo). On the other side is the image of the *Sibyl* seated by the fountain with a personification of the Aniene at her feet.

The narratives on the corresponding walls are also dedicated to the Tiburtine Sybil, now transformed into a golden image: adored and questioned by the people, and paid homage by sacrificial rites and carried in a triumphal cortege. The delicate image of *Venus of the Sea Foam*, appears on a false tapestry on the short wall, and that of the gruff *Neptune* beside it. Both refer to the two divinities who saved Ino.

Beneath the glass pavement slabs one can see the remains of a Roman villa from the 1st century B.C. discovered in 1983 during the restoration of the floors of both this room and the one adjacent.

The beautiful mosaic in black and white marble, dated to the 1st century A.D. and executed with great exactness, presents decorative motifs of originality and refinement – placed inside a geometrical framing. We note pairs of *peltae* (the shields of Amazons), the *Nodo di Salomone*, the double axe, four apples separated by crossed daggers. Inside the central geometric motif various objects are drawn (a whip, a shield, a club, a sickle), and also floral motifs (a spike of wheat and a flowering twig). The masonry revealed during the archeological excavations in 2002-03 connected all the spaces on the lower floor; this evidence, combined with what had already been seen in other areas of the palace and the garden confirmed that the ancient Roman villa was a grand and extensive complex, articulated in a series of buildings arranged in various layouts on terraces of various levels, with a great panoramic central fore-structure (including the areas with mosaic floors) which divided into two sides: one arcaded, the other, on the opposite side, with a *criptoportico*.

The Roman structures were obliterated during the construction of the Benedictine monastery and in the later Franciscan enlargement which partially exploited the terraces and the masonry, though changing orientation on its lateral walls, as can be seen beneath the windows of the large wall below the mosaic.

In the **First Tiburtine Hall** (n. **21**) one finds a version of the legend of the origins of Tivoli. In the center of the vault-

42. *Ercole combats Albio and Bergio* (fresco in the First Tiburtine Room)

43. *Volcano* (fresco in the First Tuburtine Room)

44. *The Fountain of Tivoli or Oval Fountain under construction* (fresco in the First Tuburtine Room)

45. First
Tuburtine Room

ed ceiling is the *Arrival in Lazio of the Three Greek Brothers, Tiburto, Catillo, and Corace,* and their victorious battle against the Latins. In the four compartments are the Scenes of Sacrifice offered to prepare for the foundation of the city (in one picture we see Tiburto tracing with a plough the perimeter of the site which will bear his name), as well as some moments during the *Construction of Tibur,* with the fortifications, the gates and the palaces. The stories narrated on the long walls offer analogous themes: over the fireplace is the *Battle of the Three Brothers for the Conquest of Sicletum* (called only later *Tibur*) on the walls facing this is the *Sacrifice of Thanksgiving,* depicting the three brothers after their victory.

Also in this room a minor wall is ded-

icated to the God Protector, Hercules, depicted in his Tenth Labor, when, to defend the precious herd of cattle stolen from Gerione, he wields his club against Albio and Bergio, who menace him. He is rescued by Zeus, who launches a rain of stones from heaven against his enemies. This episode bestowed upon the hero the name *Ercole Saxanus.* Completing the decorative cycle are landscapes and images of Divinities, placed in pairs inside fake niches: *Vulcano with Venus, Jupiter with Juno, Apollo with Diana,* and finally, along the window side, *Bacchus with Cerere.* Also along this wall we recognize a picture of the Fountain of Tivoli (or Oval Fountain) which Cardinal Ippolito was commissioning at the same moment below in the garden. Thus, this was a kind of "photograph"

of the Oval still under construction. The following **Hall of the Fountain** (n. **22**) leads us to the heart of the palace. In Ippolito's time, this room was used to receive guests who arrived from the garden below, but especially for convivial gatherings of poets, literati, and musicians, and temporarily made even more splendid thanks to ephemeral decorative installations.

It will hardly surprise you then to see the stage-set decoration of this room, where the very walls seem to dissolve away into an illusionary loggia, with terraces delimited by pairs of imposing twisting columns opening on wide prospects. The walls on one side are dominated by one of the most beautiful inventions of the villa: the fountain covered with multicolored mosaics with the relief of the Tiburtine acropo-

46. Hall of the Fountain

47. *Synod of the Gods* (fresco on the ceiling of the Hall of the Fountain)

lis and the temple of Sybil situated in the central niche. Folgetta recalls that during the banquets here one could hear the soft sound of the water in the fountain mixing with that of the Fountain of the Long Sleeve; "jets of water of various types, spurting from these fountains and murmuring, delighting the ears of those at the table and completing the scene.'

On the opposite wall is a *View of Villa d'Este*, taken from a low angle with the garden and the fountain still unfinished. On the long walls there are other images of the villa: the Fountain of the Organ is depicted twice – in its original version in the small picture between the door and the first window; and then in its present form in the large picture completely repainted in 1930. In a small section of the opposite wall is a rare view of Ippolito's Roman villa on the Quirinal Hill.

The decoration of the ceiling is completely taken up with mythological themes. Here inside the usual weave of grotesques (unusual, however in the delicacy of figuration), we find, inside stucco frames, *Scenes of Sacrifice* to ancient gods, flanked on the two long sides by the *Four Elements*. In the corners we

find the white eagle which alludes to Ippolito, in well-modelled stucco high relief, and flanked by pairs of gods: *Mercury and Minerva, Mars and Venus, Bacchus and Cerere, Jupiter and Juno.* According to tradition, the painter Girolamo Muziano was painted in the guise of Mercury.

At the pinnacle of the vault, a highly foreshortened fake collonade frames a kind of *velario* held up by nails along the borders, on which is painted the *Synod of the Gods*, inspired by the analogous fresco by Raphael in the Loggia of Psyche in the Villa Farnesina. Among those participating at the banquet are all the gods of Olympus, from Jupiter sitting at the center to Bachus, in the foreground mixing wine, to Apollo, placed with his lyre on the right. At the center of the composition (though seen over the shoulder) Hercules can be seen turning to look back at the viewer.

The decorative scheme of the room was developed between 1565 and 1570. In 1565, Girolamo Muziano, with a group of painters, began executing the frescoes of the ceiling, continuing then along the walls. In 1568, the Bolognese Paolo Calandrino made the fountain, completing a job already begun by Curzio Maccarone. In 1570 the landscape painter Matteo Neroni was paid to retouch the central picture of the ceiling and other (not further specified) pictures, and Il Tivolino was paid to work on the fountain. The sequence and nature of these many different commissions is the object of still active critical debates – in fact, even the Banquet of the Gods, traditionally attributed to Federico Zuccari, is increasingly offered instead to the studio of Muziano. The **Fountain** (n. **23**), is unfortunately today no longer active and has lost the "cliffs" that once formed the base of the Tiburtine lanscape depicted in the niche. Its particular fascination is due less to the rigorous framing of its design than to the modeling and the preciousness and variety of its materials. Its maker, Paolo Calandrino, used tiny rustic mosaic tiles of ancient marble, *paste vitree*, fragments of glass, shells and precious stones, not only on the front and the crown in the form of quince shoots but also on the cup held up by dolphins and below in the basin in the background inhabited by marine animals.

From the Salon one may exit onto the loggia and then descend towards the garden. We advise, on the other hand, to continue the visit of the frescoed rooms.

The ornamentation of the **Hall of Hercules**, (n. **24**) is dated to 1565-66 and ascribed to Girolamo Muziano and his

team. The pictures on the ceiling celebrate the *Labours of Hercules*. With respect to the Salon, the perspective tricks here are less flamboyant, although here, too, one can find false

48. Rustic Fountain in the Salon

49. *Hercules with the Columns* (fresco on the ceiling of the Hall of Hercules)

50. *Hercules and the Hydra* (fresco on the ceiling of the Hall of Hercules)

51. *Hercules welcomed in Olympus,* (fresco on the ceiling of the Hall of Hercules)

52. on the following page: Hall of Nobility

53. Nobility on the throne between Liberality and Gererosity (fresco on the ceiling of the Hall of Nobility)

doors and windows. However, here more weight is given to extensive panoramic landscapes, rich with mirrored lakes and enlivened by ancient architecture and rustic buildings. In much evidence, of course, are the heraldic symbols of Ippolito d'Este – an eagle circled by a golden quince branch accompanied by the motto *ab insomnia non custodita dracone.*

The ornamental articulation of the pavilion roof is more complex. It is subdivided into sectors by stucco partitions, which, in the corners are emblazoned with the Este Heraldic Crest held up by *putti.* Here too the ornamental texture presents great richness and particular vatiety in the creative workmanship of the grotesques, The figurative inserts depict images of the *Cardinal Virtues.* The theme is the *Labours of Hercules*: eight episodes are displayed on the white background of ornamental grotesques. The last four are inserted, on the other hand, in narrative contexts inside ovals which are presented by geniis and topped by emblems of the house of Este and pairs of personifications of Fame.

Continuing clockwise, we can observe: *Hercules and the Lion of Nemea, The Theft of the Cattle of Gerione* (in an oval), *The Struggle with the Hydra of Lerna, The Capture of the Bull of Minos, The Killing of the Centaur Nesso, kidnapper of Deianira* (in an oval), and the *Struggle with the Swamp Bird of Stinfalo, Hercules with the Columns,* the episode from the *Madness of Hercules who kills his Children* (in an oval), *Hercules holding the Globe of Atlantis, Hercules against the Dog Cerberus, The Struggle with the Giant Anteus* (in the oval) and the *Battle with the Centaur.* These episodes illustrating the hero victorious after his many trials constitute a natural introducton to the *Apotheosis of Hercules* painted on the center of the ceiling, where we see him welcomed among the gods of Olympus. This painting, incidently, is another one at various times attributed to either Zuccari or to the school of Muziano. The **Hall of Nobility,** (n. **25**), like the following room dedicated to Glory, does not offer particular difficulties regarding attribution. No less than Vasari (1568) described the presence of Federico Zuccari. Zuccari himself noted: "Many worked for Federigo, as happened in similar projects, so that it could be done quickly as possible, at the will of the Cardinal, who desired things to be rushed into existence." Despite the participation of various assistants, the pictorial decoration here is distinguished by formal unity and coherent execution, thanks also to the well organized architectural framework designed by Zuccari (the artist already boasted a wide experience in the figurative décor of noble palaces, most notably at Caprarola).

Ionic columns painted on marble baseboards subdivide the walls. On the short and extreme sides of the long walls, the busts of ancient philosopher appear on shelves (we find *Pythagoras, Bias,* an unidentified person, *Solon, Diogenes, Socrates, Periander,* and *Plato*), whose faces appear in front of walls

covered in fake marble with painted in-laid stones. In the middle of the walls Federico has painted false tapestries with brilliant colors, with allegories of the *Graces, Two Virtues* (perhaps Temperance and Prudence), and the *Liberal Arts*.

Thematic allegories in honor of the patron dominate even the ceiling, starting with the central painting in which *Nobility* triumphs. It is flanked by *Liberality* and *Generosity*. They form a kind of frame around the central axis with four sections: the *Diana of Ephesus*, fertility goddess so important in the iconological program of the Tiburtine villa, accompanied by a scroll *De Rerum Natura*, which appears beside a radiant Immortality. In the two ovals we are presented with: *Opulence*, surrounded by treasure and emblems of

power, and *Honor*, a regal figure before whom men are kneeling.

The decorations of the next, small **Hall of Glory**, (n. **26**) were completed between 1566 and 1567 by Federico Zuccari and eight assistants. They remain one of the most successful creations of the Roman "Maniera" due to their ability to link conceptualization of subject with lively creative inspiration and sumptuous rendering of form. Compared to its predecessor work, Zuccari uses a compositional plan that is rather complex, and he takes pleasure in extending the limited space available by using illusionistic tricks such as the putti depicted with dramatic foreshortening at the base of the ceiling, which, in turn boats the golden apples which are the emblem of the Cardinal. For at least two of these – the one seated on the sides of *Time* – the master's hand has been definitively confirmed.

On the walls, richly decorated with false marble and colored drapery, there are more openings – both real and fake – and also the sheer invention of the illusionistic shelving which reveal, behind the partially raised drapes, the presence of objects in daily use by the Cardinal (but also a Papal Tiara, alluding to Ippolito's ambition). The taste for antiquity is evident in the parade of fake ancient sculpture and in the framing device of

54. on the preceding page: Hall of Glory

55. Hall of the Hunt

56. Scene of
Naval Battle
(fresco in the
Hall of the
Hunt)

grotesques of *The Virtues (Temperence, Strength, Justice, Prudence)*. Unfortunately, the central painting of the ceiling, the *Allegory of Glory*, has been lost. Alternating on the corner panels are the *Four Seasons* are illustrations of *Religion, Fortune, Magnanimity*, and *Time*.

At the far end of the palace, there is a room which at the time of the death of the Cardinal (1572) boasted wall coverings of leather *corami* treated with silver and gold. The pictorial scheme from which the room takes its name, **Hall of the Hunt**, (n. **27**), was a product of the end of the 16th century or the beginning of the 17th. Marked with a distinct figurative style, it is less attributable to Antonio Tempesta as once suggested, than to a master with a northern provenance. The large Scenes of the Hunt, with deer and duck, joined with pairs of rustic persons in the foreground of these rural landscapes, constitute the principle subject of the pictures. There are especially delicious details in the ornamentation: naval battles, for example, and hunting trophies along the borders of the painted tapestries. Al-

so delightful is the trompe-l'oeil in the alcove of the entrance door: a little monkey chained to a vase of citrus and a dog barking at a doe.

From the Hall of the Hunt, we descend to the garden via the "snail" stairs, begun by Ippolito and completed by Luigi with the stairs in solid travertine. Originally, the stairs linked the reception rooms with the *Pallacorda Court,* pallacorda being a kind of *antelitteram* tennis which Ippolito personally introduced to Italy from the French court, where it was much in vogue. In order to astonish and delight his guests, he decided to build a facility for the new game in the recess between the palace and the Grand Loggia which, at the end of the 18th century was partially covered and used as a stable and then completely transformed during the 20th century restorations so that it could be used as a *Reception Structure* for visitors to the museum. In this recently renovated space one now finds a book shop and a cafeteria which also offers tables in the open air. Exiting through the glass doors we reach the main thoroughfare of the garden, the **Vialone**.

THE GARDENS AND THE FOUNTAINS

The tour of the garden begins with the **Vialone** (n. **1**) on the first terrace of the slope below the palace, an extraordinary viewing point of both the garden and the panorama beyond.

Ligorio's own description notes that it was 'big enough to joust in." In fact, it is the largest space in the garden, a place where, during summer evenings, in the glow of luminaries and fireworks, the Este Cardinals staged parties and games for their guests (such as the Quintana and other knightly tournaments) buffoonery of the court jesters and acrobatic spectacles.

The avenue, which extends over 200 meters in length, is closed on one end by the Fountain of Europa and on the other by the **Gran Loggia**, or "**Cenacolo**" (n. **2**) a spectacular loggia/ belvedere. The loggia "made with great design and architecture" (Zappi, 1576) was constructed between 1568 and 1569 and its decorative program was never completed. Inside, it was to be stuccoed, gilded, and adorned with "masterly paintings." (Del Re, 1611).

On the side facing the Vialone, the architecture takes on the motif of a triumphal arch and is open on the other two sides with arcades which direct the eye towards the garden and the countryside. The vast covered space thus remains always cool and ventilated offering a true refuge from the summer heat. Directly connected with the wing containing the kitchens via a covered stair, it represented for Ippolito the ideal setting for entertaining his guests in sumptuous conviviality and even today it houses a restaurant which in summer makes a most pleasant stop.

Now we walk down the Vialone, which originally was shaded by a double row of elms its entire length (with the exception of the area in front of the palace), in such a way as to not "impede

VEDVTA IN PROFILO DEL PALAZZO NEL GIARDINO ESTENSE IN TIVOLI

the view of the garden and plains and mountains of the area." (Del Re).

The principal elevation of the palace rises three floors above a high basement. To adapt the pre-existing building to its new function as background scenery for the garden and create a connection with the geometrical fabric of the entire com-

57. The Vialone beneath the Palace (etching by G.F. Venturini, 1691)
58. The Gran Loggia or "Cenacolo" behind the Vialone

59. The double
loggia of the
Palace and the
Fountain of the
Tripod

plex in conformity with the rules of the renaissance aesthetic, this side of the convent building was reworked several different times by Ippolito, and, after 1567-68, finally assumed its definitive form with the realignment of the front elevation and the widening of its side in the two fore-structures, which according to the plan, were meant to culminate in two small towers.

The external angles of the palace were done to correspond with the longitudinal lateral axis while, in the center, the loggia thrusting out represented the focal point of the principle axis of the garden.

The concept was never completed with the envisoned coat of travertine colored finish, and is barely articulated in the fore-structures and with the *marcapiano* bands. On the uniform surface of the long façade, the architecture *a serliane* of the **double loggia** (n. **3**) takes on great prominence. Realized in 1566-67 and refinished in 1568 with the internal decorations, it is constructed in travertine.

In two orders, the first Doric and the second Corinthian, it is flanked by two monumental staircases in travertine, with clear reference to Michelangelo's project for the Palazzo Senatoriale on the Capitoline Hill. A combination terrace-belvedere for the salon and the upper floor, and entrance loggia for the first floor (paved in 1571 with reused *opus sectile* and originally graced with a fountain of mixed African marble in the place of the central balustrade) it boasted a grand staircase, and a nymphaeum on the ground floor where today is found the **Fountain of Leda.**

This nymphaeum is made up of a large rectangle, articulated on the back walls with a niche containing the fountain. On the tartar cliffs there is a headless statue of *Minerva*, (found in the garden of the Palazzo Manni in Tivoli). This substitutes for the original sculptural group of *Jupiter and Leda turned into a Swan* (today at the Galleria Borghese in Rome) which was flanked

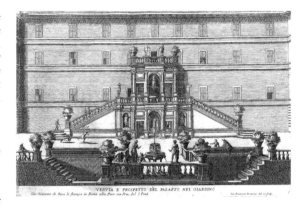

by statues of their four children, Elena and Clytemnestra in the internal niches and Castor and Pollux in the external (all sold in the 18th century). The nymphaeum was furnished with a unique hydraulic device, by which a jet, spouting from a vase held by Leda, landed upon a disc of metal and then opened into rays simulating sunbursts. At the end of the 19th century, already bare of

60. Elevation of the Palace (etching by G.F. Venturini, 1691)

61. Leda with Jupiter transformed into a swan (Galleria Borghese, Rome)

62. on the preceding page: Upper Terrace of Villa d'Este, (watercolor by E. Roesler Franz)

63. Fountain of the Tripod (etching by G. Maggi 1618)

64. Fountain of Pegasus

Fontana incontro il Palazzo   nel Giardino di Tivoli.

its original sculptural decoration and dry due to the exhaustion of the Rivellese acqueduct, it was redone in a Christian theme by Cardinal Gustav von Hohenlohe with a sculptural group in gesso now lost showing Christopher Columbus in the act of delivering the cross to America. In front of the loggia, the Vialone (Avenue) widens into a small terrace-belvedere which "serves as a viewing place for the garden," as was noted in the plans of Ligorio.

Here, around 1930, Attilio Rossi placed

the **Fountain of the Tripod** (n. **4**), a copy of an ancient basin in marble held up by a twisting central column and by three pilasters (the original today may be seen at the Louvre). The original fountain on this site, Fountain of the Sea Horses, taken from Villa Adriana by Ippolito, included also a sculptural group of horses topped by a basin supported by three dolphins (today in the Vatican Museum).

On the sides of the terrace, two double stairs lead to the Loggia of Pandora, but, if one has the time, it is well worth it to walk the entire length of the Vialone to see other fountains and grottoes on the north-east end of the garden.

On this end the scenic background of the Vialone is made up by the **Fountain of Europa** (n. **5**). This is in visual correspondence with the Gran Loggia from which it takes its overall design. This, too, is in the form of a Triumphal Arch with two overlaying orders, the first again Doric and the second Corinthian, which frame the large niche with the basin. Above the trabeation is a large convex shell between two volutes. The nymphaeum, begun at the time of Ippolito, remained incomplete at his death and was finished by the architect Matta de Rossi only in 1671.

In the center of the large niche, originally there was a sculptural group of the classical period, *Europa embracing the Bull* (now in the Villa Albani in Rome). Below the statue was a tartar *scogliera* which focused the water towards an ancient tub in *cipollino* marble (the present location of which is unknown).

Descending the ramp on the left, we reach the **Fountain of Pegasus**, (n. **6**) which stands out against the laurel woods.

At the center of the low oval basin, we find the 16th century travertine statue of the mythical Winged Horse Pegasus, in the act of landing upon Mount Elicon. With the strike of his hooves, he causes the spring of Ippocrene to burst forth, the waters of which the Muses will drink. The theme of Pegasus was re-

current in renaissance villas and conveyed the idea that the garden had become the new home of the muses, who in turn, inspired Art. The winged horse forms a scenic unity with the Oval Fountain, below, from which one can see beyond the artificial mountain of the Sybil which represents the Tiburtine mountains. Thus, once again, Ippolito's patronage is celebrated – a patronage that has brought both water and the arts to the hilltop.

Turning back, we walk down the avenue which fronts the ramp, leading us towards the **Grotto of Igea and Aesculpius** (n. 7) realized following the example of the classical nymphaeums recessed into the retaining wall of the terrace above.

Outside, the arches are ringed by a band of marbled tiles with a pattern of interlocking spirals (almost completely redone during the major restoration of 2002 on the base of the parts still *in situ*). Of the original frescoed false marble decoration which originally completed the framing of the prospects, there is only a fragment remaining in the Grotto of Igea.

The inside is covered with a layer of tar-

tar flakes, framed by bands of marbled tiles. A mosaic molding with a Greek motif runs along the perimeter and connects the two grottoes. On the back wall, a tile band with black and white spirals borders the niche, the basin of which is ornamented with a particularly well designed and preserved mosaic, this of shells made of multi-colored fragments. Begun in 1569 by Tommaso da Como, at the time of Ippolito's death the grotto housed statues of *Aesculpius,* God of Medicine (now in the Louvre) and his *daughter Igea*, Goddess of health (now in the Vatican Museum).

Walking alongside the long wall which reveals the vertical displacement between this level and the one above, we take the avenue which Ippolito, according to Zappi: "strolled saying the *offitio* with Monsignor Mureto," and therefore it has been named the **Cardinal's Walk** (n. 8). The cool, calm environment, shaded by the high wall and the many plants in the woods below, is particularly

65. Grotto of Igea and Aesculpius

66. Statue of Aesculpius (Louvre Museum, Paris)

FONTANA DETTA DELL' IDRA POSTA SOPRA À QVELLA DEL BICCHIERONE

67. Fountain of Pandora (etching by G.F. Venturini, 1691)

68. Statue of Pandora (Capitoline Museums, Rome)

enjoyable on the hottest days and seems designed to inspire meditation.

In the center of the walk, the **Loggia of Pandora** (n. **9**) forms a covered walkway, open on three sides with great arcades. In the complex system of staircases between the palace and garden, the nymphaeum serves as a kind of hub and repeats the plan "a serliane," the same role played by the loggia in front of the palace.

Inside, the recess of the fountain is delimited by two wide rectangular openings in travertine, richly outlined, on whose tops are inserted two semicircular tubs. Built between 1566 and 1568,

work took place again in 1570 when the stuccos on the roof were completed and Matero Neroni was paid to work on the niches. But already in 1572 Andrea Romano had to redo the marble and enamel tiles which Zappi described as being designed with "white eagles, lilies, and golden apples."

Due to periodic leakage from the terrace above, the gilded stuccos, the paintings on the ceiling, and the mosaics of the fountain were replaced with more durable tartar or plaster coverings in the 17th century. Of the 16th century decorations, only the tiny mosaic of the apse basic remains, with a floral motif alternating with monochrome bands; and also a wide portion of the elegant geometrical design found in the niche under layers of mineral concretions during the restoration of 2002.

Iin the niche there was originally an ancient statue found at Hadrian's Villa, this the mythical *Pandora* with a vase in her hand. Thanks to a clever hydraulic trick, water gurgled out of this vase as if representing all the evils of the world which could no longer be held in check. The statue was flanked by two statues of *Minerva* in the two niches behind the stairs (*Pandora* and one *Minerva* are today in the Capitoline Museum).

At the end of the 19th century, with the ancient statues sold off and the water no longer running, Hohenlohe transformed the nymphaeum into a chapel, installing a statue of the *Virgin seated on her throne showing the Cross to the Infant*. This was a work by Tadolini later transferred to the Coccanari Chapel in the Tivoli cemetery. During his stays in the area, Franz Liszt loved to come here to pray before the image which offered flowers from the garden and to which he dedicated a *Salve Regina* and an *Ave Maris Stella*.

Leaving the loggia we find – in front of the chalice – the spray of the **Fountain of the Bicchierone** (n. **10**).

To see it to best advantage, it is necessary to walk the path to the right, a route lined by an ancient boxwood hedge and

69. Fountain of the Bicchierone and Loggetta of the Cardinal

70. The progression of loggias along the central axis (detail from the etching by G.F. Venturini 1691)

by a pomagranate wood and then turn left towards the level path flanked by the quince orchard.

Half way down the lane we find the fountain, whose basin extends outwards in the form of a shell which reaches up to the height of the terrace above. Inside, there is a toothed chalice from which a jet of water sprays up. The modern mosaic substitutes for the original which began falling apart only a few years after its execution.

This is one of the two fountains which Gian Lorenzo Bernini created at Villa d'Este between 1660 and 1661 at the request of Cardinal Rinaldo I. Already famous and overloaded with commissions in the construction of Baroque Rome, Bernini took the time to personally supervise the ongoing construction and was paid by the Cardinal with splendid gifts, among them a ring which was worth 400 gold scudi.

The fountain was inaugurated in May of 1661 in honor of guests of the villa. The following month, Bernini, inspecting his creation, had the height of the spurting water reduced so as to not block the view from the Loggia of Pandora above. In fact, the new fountain came to interpose itself between the sequence of the various loggias sloping

VEDVTA D'VNA PARTE DELLE FONTANELLE NEL VIALONE SOPRA LA FONTANA DE DRAGHI

71. Grotto of Hercules (etching by G.F. Venturini, 1691)

72. Statue of Hercules with the boy Achilles in his arm (Louvre Museum, Paris)

along the central axis, which reveals the succession of terraces on the steep hill below the palace and thus constitutes a linking element between the volumes of palace and garden.

A small balustraded terrace, fringed by high laurel hedges, extends towards the garden in front of the fountain. It is said that this shady balcony was one of Ippolito's favorite spots. Indeed, it has even taken on the name Loggetta del Cardinale. Here Ippolito read classical poetry and took part in erudite conversation with the intellectuals in his circle, occasionally glancing around

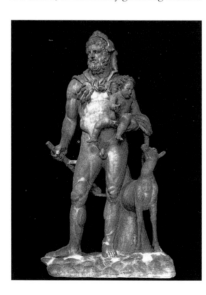

at his creation rapidly taking shape. In fact, it was only a few years after Ippolito's death that one project was completed: the arrangement on the terrace of a statue of *Hercules with the young Achilles in his arm* (now at the Louvre). The statue, turned towards the garden and set on a high pedestal behind the balustrade, was thus quite visible from below and took its place in a sequence of three statues along the central axis, all illustrating Hercules in three moments of his legend: Hercules killing the dragon Ladone, Hercules reclining in repose after his labours, and Hercules immortal, "adored dagli Huomini per Dio."

This loggeta made a terrace-roof for the **Grotto of Hercules** (n. **11**). Below the level on which one walks, there is a cistern used for the hydraulic works of the niche below and by the Fountain of the Dragons, still further down. To see the grotto, we turn right at the end of the lane, and descend the diagonal ramp lined by a forest of corbezzoli. The grotto, positioned above the Hundred Fountains (be careful not to slip here as it is always dampened by spray!) is planted on three sides and open to the valley with a great arcade which frames the niche.

The masonry structure was built by the master Tommaso da Como in 1568-69. Immediately afterwards, the stone cutters Biasioto and Raffaello Sangallo created the travertine balustrade. In 1570 Paolo Calandrino did the now lost stucco reliefs on the base of the statue of *Hercules Recumbans* (now at the Vatican Museum). This portrayed animals, or according to other sources, the labours of Hercules.

Now we once again climb the diagonal ramp on the other side, and before descending again we can make an interesting deviation entering the little lane on the right of the little square. This leads to a little belvedere from which we may appreciate the complexity of the visual organization of the Oval Fountain. To see the fountain from below, we turn

around and descend on the ramp to our right. At the end of this, we make a brief stop to observe the **Grotto of Pomona** (n. **12**). This is similar in architecture to the Grotto of Hercules and that of Flora, of which more later. All three are aligned on the same level in the area behind the Hundred Fountains. The first indicates the entrance, the second the central area, and the third the end, thus also indicating the diagonal access path in the area of the hanging forests above the avenue.

The nymphaeum here is presented to the viewer as a kind of ordered arcaded prospect, enriched with mosaics and with a frieze modeled in stucco made up of the coat of arms of Ippolito flanked by two cornacopia.

The masonry structure and the waterworks were realized at the time of Ippolito, while the mosaics, in large part lost, were from the first decades of the 17th century. All the internal surfaces in tartar and much of the mosaic of the external surfaces are ascribable, however, to the restoration of the 1930s, as indicated on an inscription. An idea of the original ornamentation is well expressed by the fragment of black and white greek mosaic visible in the lower part of the walls, inside the collecting pool,

found under layers of calcification during the restoration of 2002. Indeed, this was an important discovery: once the heavy mass of minerals were removed, the workers uncovered a spectacular classical era mask in white marble from which the waters originally flowed. This had, in fact, been cited in the documentary sources in the antiquary collections of Ippolito.

Descending some steps in front of the grotto, the view of the Hundred Fountains opens up. We will examine this in a moment, but now on our right we approach first the **Oval Fountain** (n. **13**), defined in the *Descrittione* as "the most important of all the fountains in this garden, and perhaps of all Italy." Admired by visitors of every epoch, this fountain was one of the first to be installed, done simultaneously with the organization and building of the terraces themselves, indeed it was designed as a kind of hub linking the two orthogonal slopes from which the garden was carved out and also as the place from which the waters of the Aniene, channeled by the underground aqueduct, first made their appearance. From this point, indeed, the distribution network which feeds all the fountains, begins. And from this point begins one of the two "water ways" which visually link the most representative episodes on the two extreme ends of the complex.

Designed by Pirro Ligorio, it is one of the first "water theaters," that is, a place conceived as a stage set for aquatic shows in which water is animated in a wide variety of shapes. In its architecture, it is articulated on several levels. There is a nymphaeum in the shape of a semi-circular recess, grottoes, and artificial mountains. A great oval pool extends in the back half of an arcaded semi-circle and niches inside this protect ten Nereids in stuccoed *peperino*. These are almost completely hidden by vegetation. Sculpted by Giovanni Battista della Porta in 1567 on designs by Pirro Ligorio, they hold vases from which jets

73. Mascherone in the Grotto of Pomona

74. Oval
Fountain or
Fountain of
Tivoli

75. Nereids of
the Oval
Fountain (photo
circa 1930)

of water spray out into the pool, while a theatrical series of fan-shaped sprays are emitted from vases in the arcades of the semi-circle. Other smaller jets gurgle out from bowls on the balustrade above, but the most spectacular play of water is located at the center of the semi-circle, where a thundering cascade emerges from a large crater shaped dish above which sprays water into the shape of a lily.

Above this is an artificial mountain made of *pietra spugnola*. Hidden in the "rustic clifs in the form of a half- moon theater," (Del Re), now covered in vegetation, there are purpose- built fissures built out of terra cotta, now obstructed, from which water dripped through the rocks.

At the base of the mountain three grottoes open up from which other water courses spring out, and at the center of these there is the colossal statue of *Sybilla Albunesa with her son Melicerte,* sculpted in travertine in 1568 by Gillis van den Vliete, and on the sides, two statues of the rivers *Erculaneo* and *Anio*, created by Giovanni Malanca in 1566. After tumbling down the three pools beneath the statue, the waters are collected in a canal that runs along the perimeter of the upper walkway, rimmed by a travertine balustrade reconstructed in 1926 by Attilio Rossi.

The work was begun in 1565 by the master Tomasso da Como; in 1566 the fountain maker Curzio Maccarono created the artificial rocks (in tartar) and arranged the hydraulic facility. Between 1567 and 1569 came the finishing touches: work commenced on the colossal statues and the travertine elements by Raffaello Sangallo.

In 1569, Foglietta described it as completed, but still one year later Paolo Calandrino was to actually finish the stucco and mosaic decorations in the prospect of the semi-circle, and the ceramicist Bernardino de' Gentili de Aversa ornamented the parapet of the pool with "litttle squares outfitted with multicolored glass, on which the eagle and lily were drawn," thus conforming to the plan illustrated in the *Descrittione*. One of the original panels in majolica in relief is still conserved on the right side of the pool while the rest were redone during the 1930s.

The fountain, originally called "of Tivoli" is connected – along with the Fountain of Pegasus (on the upper part of the hill behind) – to the Hundred Fountains and to the Fountain of "Rometta", by a complex iconological program created by Pirro Ligorio in harmony with certain key episodes in the life of Cardinal Ippolito. Metaphorically, this recreates the physical nature of the Tiburtine Mountains directly behind: the three statues represent the rivers of Tivoli, the rocks and artificial

grottoes reproduce its mountains and caves, the miniature waterfall alludes to the great leap of the Aniene which falls to the valley below the rocky acropolis of Tivoli, with its round temple of the Sibyl.

The place is particularly pleasant in the warmest hours of summer due to the coolness created by the great amount of water thundering about and by the shade of four majestic plane trees in the court before the fountain, the only planted elements remaining from the 16th century.

Early visitors didn't fail to describe the well-being they felt in this space when, according to Ligorio's plan, "beds were

76. Oval Fountain (etching by A. Lafrery, 1575)

77. 16th century decoration in majolica *formelle* on the parapet of the basin, Oval Fountain

78. Upper
walkway and
craters of the
Oval Fountain

placed there in the open in summer to
rest in during the day." The most ap-
preciated path was inside the dark and
damp ring-shaped *criptoportico* beside
the pool where they "sent the women

for their fun and had them splashed with
many sprays of water made with great
artifice" (Zappi) which were set off
without warning. The other most popular path was the narrow and slippery

passage beneath the veil of water from the cascade itself, now closed to the public because of danger.

You can, however, inspect the two large marble plates beside the entrance, one of which was brought here in 1612 from the church of S. Lorenzo and the other previously of slate, substituted by Mattia de Rossi in 1672 with a similar slab in marble.

On the south-east side of the enclosure, a building sunk into the embankment contains, within it, the **Grotto of Venus** (n. **14**), realized in 1565-68 on a design by Pirro Ligorio.

The central space (for years given over in concession to the Laboratorio del Papiro "Fannius" which houses the Teaching Museum of Ancient Books) has a typology traceable to the ancient nymphaeums of Sant'Antonio in Tivoli, while in the architectural imprint of the aquatic spectacle one can recognize many matrices connecting it to other Roman models.

In Ippolito's time, the grotto was used as a meeting point and place of conversation on summer afternoons because "it offered coolness due to its natural shape and delighted due to the rumbling of the fountain outside and the murmur of the one within" (Foglietta). The fountain is delimited with a large arch placed in relationship with the pool done in a form of mixed lines in travertine. The walls are scanned with a rhythmic series of flattened, decorative pilasters which frame semi-circular niches at contrasting angles, adorned with stucco shells in the basins and by vases which support tiny tartar *scogliere* (sea reefs) in the form of baskets of fruit. In the center of the water play, an arch frames the large niche which contains a large sea grotto in Tiburtine tartar.

All the walls were adorned with polychrome decorations in multiple materials, in large part conserved if degraded and covered with thick mineral deposits (scale) caused by the steady stream of water from the embankment above. The niches and vases are decorated with bands of geometrical motifs in tartar flakes, *lapillo* and marbled tiles. The lunette above includes painted monochrome murals with grotesque figures and the arch conserves the pictorial decorations of fake marble squares.

On the other hand, there is nothing left now of the sculptural decoration which once enriched the central *scogliera*, (where there is now a virile head of unknown origin) with an ancient nude Venus, of the same type as the Capitoline Venus, flanked by two putti who embraced her.

Leaving the grotto, we observe the two **Fountains of Bacchus** (n. **15**) in the walls opposite the Oval Fountain. These were created in 1568-69.

In both, the central niche is flanked by free standing columns on tall pedestals, which on the fountain on the right are shaped like tree trunks with the stumps of cut branches, a motif that was frequently found in the rustic style, while in the other (on the left) are smooth faced rustications.

In the original layout, the niches contained two statues of Bacchus in stuccoed *peperino*.

They were removed in the 17th century and replaced with the present ones, in stucco, by now reduced to a state of

79. Grotto of Venus (etching by G.F. Venturini, 1691)

FONTANA DI BACCO IN VNA STANZA CONTIGVA AL FONTANONE NEL PIANO DELLE FONTANELLE

80. Hundred
Fountains

ruin because of the continual action of the water.

Exiting by the principle gate of the enclosure, we continue down the long avenue that cuts transversely across the garden, (around 130 meters in total) linking the Fountain of Tivoli or Oval Fountain with the Fountain of Rome, or Rometta.

The avenue is flanked on the hillside by the many streams of the **Hundred Fountains** (n. **16**) (in reality the number of water spouts here is nearly three times that amount). This is formed by three overlaying canals, surmounted by a sequence of water plays.

Along the edge of the upper canal there is a rhythmic alternation between the lilies of France, behind which rise other spurts – and the Este eagle, with a boat and obelisk – both outfitted with fan-shaped sprays. The water flows into the canal through gutters positioned between the plinths, from here it pours again into the lower canal through little channels inserted in the mouths of masks which decorated the external parapet.

The thick growth of maidenhair ferns which covers all the surfaces and the thick deposits of scale which cover the raised surfaces make it difficult to fully appreciate the remaining original stucco decoration.

The documentary sources attest that in Ippolito's time, the upper canal was crowned with twenty-two little boats alternating with seventy-two terracotta vases arranged in groups of three. In these were planted pomagranate, melangoli, and lemoncello. The areas below were decorated with elaborate stucco

frames, with *erme*, volutes, and roses. There were also panels with scenes in bas-relief inspired by Ovid's *Metamorphosis*. Along the edge of the middle canal, between the mouths of the biomorphic masks, was a succession of mosaic decorations with images of fish, birds, and sea monsters.

The work began in 1569 with the arrival of the masons, who were followed, between 1566 and 1569 by the stone-cutters who did the slabs which covered the edges of the canals, and by fountain-makers, stucco-workers, and mosaicists who did the hydraulic plays and the molded decorations. The labors were extended until 1571 with various commissions given to the sculptor Luca Antonio Figoli da Cagli for the panels of the *Metamorphosis*.

In 1622, Cardinal Alessandro commissioned a restoration of the nymphaeum, already compromised by the devastating effect of the water: the stucco reliefs were redone, and the succession of vases and boats – with the insertion of eagles flanked by lilies in the place of some groups of vases.

In 1629-1630 it was again necessary to intervene on several panels from the Metamorphosis, which were reconstructed by Giovanni Venciglia. A final 17th century restoration was noted in 1685, as recorded on the marble inscription at the beginning of the avenue; this by Duke Francesco II. On this occasion, the decorative installation of the nymphaeum was again modified and it now took on its contemporary configuration as a result of the substitution of the remaining groups of vases with groups of obelisks and lilies rotated towards the horizontal.

After centuries of abandonment, a substantial restoration was executed around 1930 by Attilio Rossi, who brought back the missing eagles and lilies with cement casts and paved the avenue, originally a dirt track, but now done with a mosaic of ancient marble.

The typology of the fountain, with its long rectilinear pools and the multiplicity of its water spouts, is traceable to the model of the nymphaeums "a facciata" of Greco-Roman tradition, common for public fountains and largely brought back into use during the middle-ages (as in the 99 Cannelle, in Aquila) and in the Renaissance. As the Oval Fountain is meant to represent Tivoli, the triple canals of the Hundred Fountains allude to the water courses and aqueducts which feed into Rome from the surrounding Tiburtine countryside.

The symbolic meaning was clearer in the 16th century array, when the only boat to travel along the upper canal "in a manner in which it really seemed to sail" according to the *Descrittione* – exactly in the direction of the Eternal City. The fountain, even without its rich decorative vestments and now overgrown, is still an extraordinarily evocative sight which has inspired painters and poets, among them, Gabriele D'Annunzio: "'midst that virgin verdure the Hundred Fountains / (soft and low like feminine mouths) speak while with splendor the sun cloaks purple, / shining (oh Glory of the Este!) on the eagle and the lily." (*Roman Elegies*)

Turning back, we now head towards the **Fountain of the Organ** (n. **17**), climbing a section of the path that leads to the gate of Piazza Campitelli and then opens onto the lane on the left that flanks the apse of S. Pietro and is framed

81. Hundred Fountains and Grotto of Pomona (etching by G.F. Venturini, 1691)

82. View of the level Gardens and the Fishponds from the terrace before the Fountain of the Organ

by two ancient columns of Portasanta marble, taken from Villa Adriana in 1613.

The viewing area in front offers a wide panorama of the lower part of the garden, with the Fish Ponds and the sprays from the Fountain of Neptune. Behind the open space, once shaded by plane trees, rises – behind the houses of the Campitelli district – the water show with a structure of a triumphal arch which hides the "*castellum aquae*" behind. The fountain was named originally the "Fountain of the Flood" or "Mother Nature," but already only a few years after its construction it took on the name of the hydraulic mechanism inserted inside it which immediately became famous in all Europe.

The work began in 1566 with the masonry structure; thereafter came the

French Fountain maker Luc Leclerc, in collaboration with his nephew Claude Venard who took over after the uncle's death, in 1568. In October 1569, the statue of *Mother Nature* or *Ephesian Diana* was raised. The fountain's decoration was still not finished, however, at Ippolito's death, even if the hydraulic works and the organ (invented by Claude Venard and installed in 1571) were already functioning.

The architectural make-up of this incomplete 16th century prospect is the one which comes down to us today, although the molded decorations were limited to the busts of *four telamoni*, sculpted in travertine by Pirrino del Gagliardo. Cornices, niches, and lunettes were still left *sans* the "gold inlaid with marble" described by Del Re, and without their mirrors which "shone

and rendered the reverberation of the setting sun." The central niche in the place of the kiosk once housed a rock *scogliera* with a central cavity that offered a view of the 22 pipes of the organ, a composition that would be imitated both at Pratolino and on the Quirinale. In front of the *scogliera*, a statue of *Mother Nature* was placed, the base of which was decorated with bas-reliefs of animals.

Even before it was completed, the fountain offered an astonishing spectacle which enchanted Pope Gregory XI-II,who visited in September, 1572. The Tiburtine historian Zappi, who witnessed the visit, attests that the Pope, the Cardinals and the Princes who accompanied him "could not believe that this organ made sounds solely as a result of the action of the water, but that there must have been somebody inside." As a result, they insisted upon speaking with the inventor Venard and upon seeing the mechanism to verify that really there was nobody.

The hydraulic organ was an absolute novelty, the first in modern times to perfect the techniques and the automatisms of the Hellenistic-Roman models described in the tracts of Erone da Allesandria and of Vetruvius, with a basic innovation that allowed complete automation: the air which produced the sounds derived not from the pressure of the water in a water tight tank, as in the ancient models, but from the separation of a an air-water mixture, a system quickly copied in many villas both in Italy and across Europe.

The water was channeled through the terrace above the *castellum aquae* be-

83. Fountain of the Organ

84. View of the hydraulic organ inside the kiosk

hind the fountain and then through a tank where it passed through strong whirlpools which captured the air, then descending through a vertical tube, finally entering the "camera aeolia" or wind chamber. This hollow space, also called the "wind well," was a water tight space where the water, falling violently, struck a slab of stone, thus causing the separation of the two elements: the water exiting was channeled towards a hydraulic wheel which then caused a toothed cylinder to move. This, as in a carillon, commanded the valves of the 22 organ pipes to open. The air was then collected in a lead pipe and reached the *somiere*, which distributed the wind to the pipes.

But the organ was not the only hydraulic device of the fountain that was created by the two brilliant French engineers to create an extraordinary exhibition of water and sound. The show began with the sound of two trumpets held up by Fame above the cornice. After this, the organ sounded – probably a madrigal of four or five voices and, after the music, there occurred the most theatrical effect of the show: the "flood." Suddenly a great spray of water tumbled

down from above – pouring from a myriad of taps placed along the cornice of the first order and in other places in view. At the same time, other tall jets spurted up from below. The great amount of nebulized water would – depending on the time of day – produce a rainbow, just as today one may often see in the spray of the Fountain of Neptune.

Towards the end of the flood, accompanied by the thunder of the crashing water, a triton placed in the fountain's pool began to sound a *buccina* (an ancient horn), first softly, then very loud, then growing softer again, as if it were moving away.

After several decades this ornate show was largely abandoned. The organ – except for the pipes – being inside the wind chamber was in close contact with water and thus its delicate mechanism suffered badly. The "flood" required constant maintenance and cleaning of the tubes which were frequently blocked by mineral deposits, and the entire installation was rapidly degraded by the frequent inundations.

In the first decades of the 17th century, by command of Cardinal Alessandro d'Este, the fountain was restored and its decorations renovated. Atop the frontispiece, between the volutes and the divided tympanum, the coat of arms with the Este Eagle was installed. In the niches of the first order the stucco statues of *Apollo* and *Orpheus* were placed. The second order was enriched with the addition of the *Caryatids in the shape of Sirens*, the *Winged Victories*, on the plumes of the big arch and by stucco bas reliefs with the scene of *Orpheus who entrances the animals* and by the *Musical contest between Apollo and Marsia* on the lateral lunettes.

At the base of the monumental water theater, itself completely redecorated with pictures in fake marble (geometrical motifs, masks and plant motifs) a pool of mixed lines was built which contains the small, elegant balustraded terrace.

Even the organ was redone – by Curzio Donati – who enlarged its musical capacity by giving it a keyboard and augmenting the registers. It was decided also to rearrange the architecture of the organ to protect it from both the water itself and from acts of vandalism. In the large niche, both the *scogliera* and the statue of Mother Nature (which we will see shortly on the level garden), and, in their place, the octagonal kiosk was created, along with the double *cupola loricata* which shields it from the elements. The organ was repaired many times in the 17th century, but by the end of the 18th, it was irremediably lost.

In 2003, after concluding a lengthy restoration, the organ was brought back into operation with a pneumo-hydraulic apparatus based on its 17th century conformation. This was done thanks to studies by Leonardo Lombardi, Patrizio Barbieri,, and to the execution by Rodney Bricoe.

Certain elements of the original construction were retained. These include the wind chamber and the tank for the production of whirlpools, while the organ itself was constructed *ex novo* with modern materials resistant to decay but consistent in their fundamental characteristics to the ancient instrument.

From the wind chamber the air enters into a *somiere* which distributes it into 144 pipes. A phono-tactile reel, activated by a hydraulic wheel, opens the pipes according to the musical requirements. The reel, through a spring and a gear, moves sideways to permit the activation of a new series of notes. Thus it is possible to insert into the reel four different pieces of music from the late renaissance.

About four minutes after the concert, the reel returns to its original position and the music begins again.

Lacking information about the original music, four late renaissance pieces have been inserted into the cylinder: *Saltarello*, by Tilman Susato (1551), *La Romanesca*, by Antonio Valente (1575), *La Shy Myze*, (anonymous, 16th century),

and *La Donna Cella* (anonymous, 16th century).

A second phono-tactile cylinder has also been constructed with four other musical pieces to use in case of breakdown or to periodically change the music: *Song known as the Dulcalina- Variazino* by Antonio Soderini (end of 16th century), *Suite di falsi bordoni* (anonymous, 1557) *Partite sopra la aria della folia da Espagna* by Bernardo Pasquini (second half of the 17th century) *Ciaccona, "Acceso mio'core"* by Francesco Mannelli (1595- before 1667).

Left of the space surrounding the Or-

85. Orpheus soothes the animals (bas relief in the Fountain of the Organ)

86. Detail of the large niche and cupola of the kiosk of the Fountain of the Organ

87. Fountain of Venus on the level of the Organ (etching by G.F. Venturini, 1691)

gan we find a balcony ringed by chairs and covered with a pergola of wisteria. This forms the backdrop for the **Fountain of Venus (n. 18)**

Realized at the beginning of the 17th century, it brought to closure – together with the adjacent "garden of melangolis' – the arrangement of the area left incomplete at the time of Ippolito's death. The nymphaeum presents a double facade, one towards the balconade and the other towards the "garden of melangolis." In the principle view, the niche is framed by two Doric semi-columns which rest on pedestals. These were once decorated with Este Eagles in bas-relief (only the one on the left remains). Along the arch the niche is framed with a molded band, while below, the *specchiatura* is decorated with bas-relief of volutes of acanthus leaves and rosettes covered with marble grains and crushed *paste vitree*. Traces of precious coverings can be found under the arch, with festoons, floral patterns and rosettes made of shells, while on the lateral pilasters pictures of human figures and vegetable life still are visible. In the restoration of 1930, the decorations were substituted by tartar coverings and the original pool and pavement were modified.

Nothing remains of the ancient array of decorative and art objects, which included a statue of *Venus* reclining on the rocks with a vase from which water sprayed out, and in the side niches, two

small *Satyrs*, while on the wall in back there were paintings "a grafitto" of the **Three Graces**.

Turning around, descending the ramp of S. Pietro, we turn right by the lane lined by hedges of myrtle and issopo which leads to the **Grottoes of the Sibyls (n. 19)**. Before the display of high flying water from the Fountain of Neptune, below (clearly visible from the two tower-belvederes on the sides), three dark caverns open to us. They are carved into the roofed structure which supports the terraces of the Fountain of the Organ. Ligorio's plan included nine grottoes "dedicated to the Sybils to honor to the highest: the Tiburtine Sybil," which was to have been decorated with "the ancient statues of the Sibyls and various paintings of marine elements." Three were actually made, but they remained incomplete after Ippolito's death.

The grottoes continue in the rectangular structure, with barrel vaults and a water display in the niche built into the back wall, the model for the underground nymphaeums of Sant'Antonio at Tivoli, an idea experimented with at various times by Pirro Ligorio at Villa d'Este.

The central chamber presents an unusual feature: at the center of the large niche there is a rectangular aperture (partly closed by mineral deposits and hidden by a veil of water). This aperture is itself submerged in a small hollow in the back which originally acted as a "wind chamber" which produced air pressure so that the trident made sounds and produced animal cries. Appropriately, Mother Nature was visible in the Fountain of the Organ, above. In fact the grottoes are actually tightly connected to the Fountain of the Organ both in symbolic terms and also in their water play. For example, the "Flood" at the end of the organ's musical presentation hid the view of the fountain and this was followed by the waterfall which poured over the *scogliera* – likewise here a veil of water hides the view of the grot-

FONTANA DI VENERE POSTA NEL PIANO DELL'ORGANO

88. Grottoes of
the Sibyls and
the spouts of the
Fountain of
Neptune

toes, pouring out from the upper canals while a virtual cataract flooded out of the "wind chamber" in the central grotto at the end of the music of the triton, falling over the cliffs below.

The water plays had already ceased their activity at the beginning of the 17th century following modifications made by Cardinal Alessandro to the Fountain of the Organ which destroyed the conduits connecting the two nymphaeums. The structures were again modified in 1661 for the construction of the Waterfall by Gian Lorenzo Bernini which included the construction of an arcade-buttress and the reinforcement of the masonry requiring both the construction of a butttressed retaining wall on top of the original and also the lowering of the tree entrance arches.

Leaving behind the spectacles of music and water linked to the mythical figures of the Tiburtine Sybil and Mother Nature, another extraordinary invention joining water, architecture, and sound induced the renaissance visitor to continue along the path of S. Pietro which crossed half way up the slope for the entire length of the garden, orienting him with a high, luminous plume and spark-

ing curiosity with strange blasts, booms and rumblings.

We, too, feel this calling, even if not tempted by strange sounds, as we walk the path downhill and continue along the level avenue to stand before the source of so many "marvels," the **Fountain of the Dragons** (n. **20**) situated along the central axis of the complex, of which it forms the true baricentric pole, connecting the vertical displacement between transverse axes of the avenue of S. Pietro (or of the Dragon) and the avenue above: that of the Hundred Fountains.

The fountain is contained within a space delimited by two facing curved ramped walkways, each two levels in height. The walls, banded by pilasters in relief, present fields clothed in tartar, delimited by mosaic bands and lines of majolica *formelle*. In the middle, a large niche is flanked by ionic columns and topped by a travertine balustrade. Along the sides, in correspondence with the landings of the curved stepped walkways, two niches framed by pilasters in relief contain basins in part still conserving their ancient mosaics.

In the middle of this architecturally de-

89. Pool of the
Fountain of the
Dragons

limited space, there is a large pool incorporating both curved and rectilinear elements. In it we find dolphins and in the center a *scogliera* supports the sculptural group of the Four Dragons. From the jaws of the dragons, powerful spouts shoot up and at the center the main jet is truly powerful, rising high with great violence. Adding to the crashing of the water in the central pool are long curving jets that emerge from vases on the internal parapets of the two curving ramped walkways. In these, two rivulets

generated high up by the breasts of two sphinxes – half woman, half winged sea horse – stream down over stucco shells and at the end of the first ramp, enter a frog, then reemerge in the second through the jaws of a salamander.

The extraordinary display of the water in this "pulcherrimae piscinae theatrum" (Kirchner) is accentuated by the backlighting and the contrast of the dark, ancient cypresses (planted in the 17th century) of which, unfortunately, only a few remain. The high spurting

fountain, visible even at the lower entrance to the garden, is the focal point of a visual prospect along the principle axis of the complex which leads the eye of the visitor up towards the series of loggias. The idea of a powerful jet in the middle of garden – seen from far away – would later be developed in the great European gardens of the 17th and 18th centuries.

Though the spectacular water plays invented by Tommaso Ghinucci remain intact, the sound effects that accompanied them have been lost. These, one of the "marvels" of the garden, consisted of a complex system which varied the water pressure, producing an intermittent eruption from the jets – explosions which were compared to artillery fire or fireworks with rumblings similar to the blasts of bombs.

The sprays themselves could be altered to produce "the appearance of a pavilion representing heavy rain, a marvelous thing to see and the same water could suddenly make beautiful changes." (Del Re). In a letter written in 1620, Fulvio Testi expressed his amazement at the metamorphoses visible here, which could change from the sound of " milky fountains, to a scene of military assault, and a violent storm." Indeed it seemed a veritable war of the elements: "Human ingenuity has upset the elements and given to water the effect of fire."

The sound of war, according to Ligorio's plans, was intended to relate to the symbolic theme of the fountain, epicenter of the representation of the myth of Hercules. The explosions and blasts were intended to induce fear in the visitors and prepare them to observe the triumph of Hercules over the Dragon Ladone, defeated bearer of the apples from the Garden of the Hesperides. In the large niche, Ligorio had intended to place a statue of *Hercules with his club*, taking on his role, according to the *Descrittione*, as "Protector of the Eagle who, killing the dragon, alludes to the Cardinal's own work, an Eagle with a branch of the apples from the Hes-

FONTANA DE DRAGHI DETTA LA GIRANDOLA SOTTO IL VIALONE DELLE FONTANELLE

perides and the motto *ab insonni non custodita dracone*. Similarly, the other statue proposed for the site: the *Gladiators* "caretakers of the fountains," and the two "military gods," *Mars* and *Perseus*, were intended to recall the martial character of the water theme here in order to create a visual unity around the figure of Hercules.

In occasion of the visit of Gregory XIII in 1572, the initial design was modi-

90. Fountain of the Dragons (etching by G.F. Venturini, 1691)

91. Sculptural group if winged dragons

92. The
fishponds and
the sea in the
original plans
(detail of the
etching by E.
Duperac, 1573)

fied in his honor and the sculptural group at the center of the pool was altered so that, instead of the Dragon Ladone with one hundred heads, there appeared the four winged dragons, emblem of the pope.

Three months later, upon Ippolito's death, the fountain was still not finished. The ramped walkways remained only partially complete, the surfaces of the semi-circle barren, the sculptural array not yet in place.

Only at the beginning of the 17th century was the decorative program completed. The central niche was then finally adorned with a marble statue – not Hercules, but instead, Jupiter seated on his throne with lightning bolts in his hand, with the roar of the water acting now as thunder. The walls were stuccoed and decorated with mosaics and polychrome pictures "*a graffito*" with the stories of Jupiter realized by Giulio Calderoni which lasted but a few years and were replaced with a finish of tartar flakes.

In the restorations of 2000-2001 an interesting discovery was made on the external walls of the ramped walkways, Here, under thick layers of mineral deposits, were found large sections of 17th century murals described in the documents as "false compartments made of wood, with a background of fake roses, with pieces of stone mixed in." The walkway in front presented on its lower walls the motif of the water chain that flowed from the external parapets of the Fountain of the Dragons, from which the water was fed (and thus not in service when, especially during the fall and winter, the upper flow was shut off).

Descending the ramp, we reach the Garden Level, preceded by three **Fish Ponds** (n. **21**), arranged along the transverse axis, which is configured like a great "street of water" (visitors are asked to hold their children by the hand, because here the barriers are low and the pools are more than four meters deep).

According to Pirro Ligorio's plans, the waters were to flow from the Fountain of the Organ through the Fish Ponds, on the opposite side of the complex, into the Fountain of the Seas, which was still not constructed. The two external pools were conceived as great parterres of water, subdivided into sectors and crossed by a little path which arrived in the middle by a little bridge "artfully built, so that one could drop into the water without danger." In the middle of the central pool, surrounded by *ermes* which shot out streams of water, two conical structures were planned: these were to be similar to the Roman fountain of the *Meta Sudans* near the Coliseum or to the *Mete* positioned near the end of the tracks of ancient hippodromes.

The work, initiated in 1563-64, simultaneously with the laying of the lower terraces, was not completed according to Ligorio's plans. Upon Ippolito's death, in 1572, only two pools were completed and the third barely begun. In the 16th century conformation, along the borders of the Fish Ponds (inhabited by swans, Indian ducks and many species of fish which served the kitchens of the Cardinal), there arose sixteen tall pilasters in the shape of *ermes*, the insides of which contained lead pipes. Above them, plumes of fan shaped spray "rushing with great impetus, was thrown high by the narrowness of the tubes so that it fell back in curves and slowly, in tiny drops dispersed, and like

rain, fell back into the pool with delicious whispers, offering a beautiful display to whomever sees it from far away or from below, as if from every part of the inside there arose cupolas of water, sometimes even covering the whole fishpond." (Foglietta). The marvels of the water were accompanied by fantasmagoric iridescent light effects which struck Montaigne: "The sun beating down generated both in the background and in the air and everywhere a rainbow which need not fear comparison with those found in the sky."

We remind the reader that rainbows were also produced in the Fountain of the Organ during the "Flood" and also in the cascades which descended from the Grotto of the Sybil. We can well imagine the astonishment this produced in the 17th century visitor, arriving at the "street of water," which was the first "marvel" to be encountered from the lower entrance of the garden.

The metamorphosis of the water along the transverse axis was intended to symbolize the perennial cycle of nature. We see the water springing from Mother Earth (Fountain of the Organ), landing in the ocean (Fountain of the Sea), after having carved out underground channels and having created waterfalls (Grottoes of the Sybils), then being flung down rivers and streams and flung into the air in vapor and condensing in beneficent showers of rain (Fish Ponds). In the first decades of the 17th century, the masonry structures and the hydraulic installations were already in decay. In 1632, the Duke of Modena, Francesco I, commissioned a reconstruction from the architect Francesco Peperelli, who was responsible also for completing the third fish pond. These

93. View of the transverse axis of the Fishponds closed off by the Fountains of Neptune and of the Organ

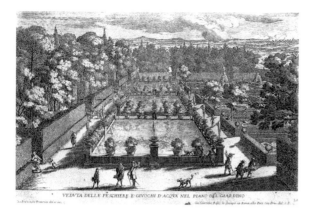

* VEDVTA DELLE PESCHIERE E·GIVOCHI D·ACQVA NEL PIANO DEL GIARDINO *

94. Axis of the Fishponds at the end of the 17th C. (etching by G.F. Venturini, 1691)

works were commemorated in a marble inscription placed on the parapet of one of the two central tanks.

The complex was completely modified: the sixteen pilasters along the perimeter were substituted with eight pedestals surmounted by vases from which the water rose in short plumes which partly fell back into the pools. Between the pilasters, twenty-four vases containing various citrus plants were installed. With the disappearance of the fantastic and ever-changing water architecture, the Fish Ponds assumed the physiognomy of a single large canal, if divided into two crossings. On the still waters of the three flat pools, one can see all the way to the Fountain of the Organ without obstructions. That fountain – seen from this point – seems to cast its plume up to the sky, to the clouds, to the greenery.

We now walk one of the avenues that flank the Fish Ponds and reach the **Fountain of Neptune** (n. **22**). This is the most imposing water display – as well as the only one – created in the 20th century. It transformed the Cascades of Gian Lorenzo Bernini. The cliff beneath the terraces of the organ had undergone a partial repair in the 16th century with the realization of the Grottoes of the Sibyls, but Ligorio's plan to replace the steep slope below with a rectilinear façade remained incomplete. This would have been articulated in two or-

ders flanked by a steep ramp linking it with the last fish pond.

In 1661, Cardinal Rinaldo I engaged Bernini to complete the work, creating a scenic background for the axis seen from the Fish Ponds. Inspired by the *genius loci*, he came up with a plan to build a waterfall which, falling from the precincts of the organ, leaped over the facing balcony of the Grottoes of the Sibyls on a bridge, then fell along the rocky crags of the slope into a lake marked by rock reefs – into which also flowed two lateral cascades.

For the construction of the cascades, it was necessary to reinforce the foundations of the terraces. A new framework inside the degraded shelving was built and then covered with rocks and vegetation artfully arranged to finally reveal a landscape that represented the Tiburtine region with its myriad of waterfalls and cascades.

Bernini was actively involved with the construction phase of the project, ordering modifications of the fountains if he wasn't satisfied. Under his personal supervision, he constructed a provisional structure with planks, rocks, and mire taken from the Fish Ponds, by which he could test the effects of the cascades, after which he wrote to Cardinal Rinaldo I: "so magnificent the site and so great the sound it creates, that it I believe it will be worthy of the exquisite taste of V.A."

Bernini's cascades, seen in the etchings of Venturini and in the drawings of Fragonard, remained a model until the 18th century, from Caserta to the English landscape gardens.

In the first decades of the 20th century, after two centuries of neglect, the cascades and their structure were in a state of decay, buried under a web of mulch and brambles.

Around 1930, Attilio Rossi – with the collaboration of the engineer Emo Salvatti, rearranged the cliff between the organ and the fish ponds, creating the present Fountain of Nepture, which incorporates the remains of Bernini's cas-

VEDVTA DELLA CASCATA SOTTO L'ORGANO NEL PIANO DEL GIARDINO

96. The
Waterfall of
G.L. Bernini
beneath the
Fountain of the
Organ (etching
by G.F.
Venturini 1691)

97. "The Garden
of the Simple"
and the 17th
century pergolas
(detail of the
etching by E,
Duperac, 1573)

cades, limited, however, to some sections of the wall's framework still visible in the central buttressing.

On the sides of the cascades, in front of the Grottoes of the Sibyls, rectilinear pools with reliefs were arrayed; from these six powerful jets of water rose from each, growing taller towards the center. The last leap from the waterfall fell in front of a grotto that featured the colossal torso of the statue of Neptune, intended in the 16th century for the unrealized Fountain of the Seas. Other violent jets open in fan shapes from the two tubs on the sides of the grotto, from where the water drains into a wider tub to then flow into a low pool with a composition that suggests the rapids of a riv-

er. There is a strong formal relationship of this fountain to the Fountain of the Organ above, which can be seen in the echoing of the mixed lines of the pool of the lower tub and also in the conceptual connection in the step-like arrangement of the twelve spouts of water, which evoke the memory of the hydraulic organ pipes, then lost.

This extraordinary nymphaeum of an *art deco* taste which still respects the *genius loci*, has, over time, become the most noted and popular image of the villa. Turning back along the little lane that flanks on its right the fish ponds, we encounter – inside a grassy flower bed – a small fountain slightly sunken into the earth. This is part of the **Fountains of the Este Eagle** (n. **23**) which in its contemporary context (that is to say after the transformations of the 19th and 20th centuries) have found themselves placed on the fringes of the squares that surround the Rotonda of the Cypresses and have lost their ancient connection with the general design of the Garden Level. The little fountains 'from pots in the shape of an octagon from inside and outside, wandering and different" (Del Re) are made up of small low pools of mixed lines in travertine, at the center of which we find sculptural groups of various types, from which the jets of water shoot up.

Now we turn to the right, on the Avenue corresponding to the central longitudinal axis, to arrive at the **Rotonda of the Cypresses** (n. **24**).

In the 16th century, at the center of the lower terrace, there had been a "Garden of the Simple," made up of sixteen square flower beds cultivated with medicinal herbs, flowers, and fruit trees subdivided into groups of four by the arms of a wooden pergola that crossed in a great octagonal pavilion. This was covered by a cupola decorated inside with eight Este eagles in silver and by a gilded lily on the crown. In the pavilion, constructed in 1570, there were interwoven trellises of grapes, heather, and jasmine.

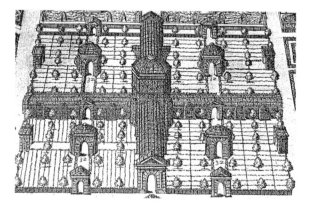

Inside there were four little fountains in the form of flowers (*fioroni*), executed in stucco by Paolo Calandrino, into which the water spurted out from above and then flowed from leaf to leaf until finally collecting in the little squared pools on the ground level, the only parts that remain visible. At the beginning of the 17th century, the wooden structures of the pergolas and pavilion, decayed and outmoded, were demolished and this freed up again the view along the

98. 17th century cypresses of the Rotonda (Photo: I. Barisi)

longitudinal axis which took the name the "Avenue of the Prospect." Even today, from the lower entrance, the garden is entirely visible from here, like in a painting, with the succession of terraces upon terraces that rise along the slope to culminate in the palace, placed "so high as to almost have its foundations in the air," (Fulvio Testi, 1620). To accentuate the base line of the prospect with its vertical counterpoint, at that time a crown of sixteen cypresses was planted so that they would again create a shady place that would enclose the four fountains with the *fioroni*. These were flanked by little tubs behind which eight statues of the *Liberal Arts* were placed on pedestals. These have been since lost. As with the former pavilion, this landscape architecture using plants has become the focal point and dominating element in the design of the garden level.

From the 16th century 'theater of Cypresses" there survives only two majestic specimens with enormous branches, true living monuments. The other cypresses now visible were planted some twenty-odd years ago, as was the laurel hedge that now reveals again the original design. The pavement, also of the same vintage, uses the original design, reconstructed on the base of a few fragments found beneath the pathway.

The ancient cypresses of Villa d'Este have inspired artists of every period, such as Franz Lizst and Gabriele d"Annunzio:

> The tallest and darkest
> Cypress of Villa d'Este
> After twilight,
> When the fountain
> Removes the veil from the maidenhair
> And from her ears
> To inspire with the distant sound
> Of the Tiburtine cascade.
> (from Nocturn)

On the right slope on axis with the transverse lane, we find the **Little Rustic Fountain** (n. **25**) in *pietra spugnola* that bears in its niche the 16th century *peperino* statue of *Winter*, originally lo-

cated in the Gran Loggia. We walk along the ring path and then turn right towards a long corridor crowned by a metal pergola, a memorial to the 16th century circle of illuminati, planted with Tiburtine grapes. This leads to the lower entrance of the garden on the via del Colle, the ancient via Tiburtina. In the center of the high walls which delimit the vestibule there are – one in front of the other – two **Rustic Fountains** (n. **26**).

Equal in size and structure, they are different in materials and construction technique from rustic works. Both have the recess of their niches framed with an arch to simulate a natural grotto created in the living rock.

Below, a semi-circular pool delimited by a wall in tartar flakes gathers the three rivulets which flow from the sides and center along the rock reef of the niche. A small water spout in the center of the pool completes the aquatic display.

In the right grotto the structure is composed of large tartar elements in the form of stalagmites, almost as if they were actual mineral deposits, while on the left it is formed from blocks of limestone barely worked on, placed in irregular horizontal lines and alternating between blocks which protrude or recede from the norm, as if this were a kind of primordial rustic order.

Executed in 1568-69 by Tomasso da Como, they were completed by the time of Ippolito's death, though still lacking the colossal statures of two monstrous giants to guard the entrance. A similar idea, likewise never realized, was proposed by the fountain maker Cuzio Donati in 1619, with two self-propelled wood statues which were to aim their muskets following the movements of the visitors.

Turning back and to the right along the enclosure wall covered with a trellis with ancient varieties of roses (in May don't forget to pause here), we arrive at the **Fountain of the Diana of Ephesus** (n. **27**) created at the beginning of the 17th century as part of the general overhaul of the Garden level commissioned by Alessandro d'Este.

For the new fountain (placed at the end of the lateral longitudinal axis), the travertine statue that had been removed in 1611 from her primitive placement in the Fountain of the Organ was put to better use. Sculpted by Gillis van den Vliete in 1568 and inspired by the famous Diana of Ephesus (2nd century A.d, once in the Farnese collection and now in the National Museum of Naples) it symbolized "**Mother Nature**."

In the 17th century layout, the statue, having lost all connection with its original iconological program, has assumed a purely decorative role as background. In relatively poor condition, the statue is placed beneath an arch made of tartar, simulating a grotto with a back-

ground also of tartar – but these are smaller flakes. From the statue's many breasts, small jets of water emerge that flow down into the low mixed-line pool. On the sides, the tartar *scogliera* divides into three little spiraling channels through which little streams of water descend.

We continue up the avenue on axis with the fountain; this is surrounded by ancient boxwood hedges and laurel. Arriving at the round piazza, we turn right along the transverse lane.

This area, like all the Garden Level, has lost its original compartmentalized design, a design which characterized it at least until the second half of the 19th century. In the 16th century configuration, on the sides of the lane there were two labyrinths with wooden frames on

99. Fountain of Diana of Ephesus or "Mother Nature"

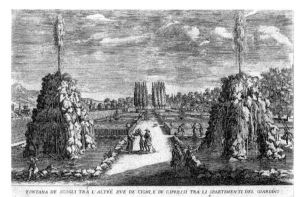

FONTANA DE SCOGLI TRA L'ALTRE DVE DE CIGNI, E DE CIPRESSI TRA LI SPARTIMENTI DEL GIARDINO

Gio Francesco Venturini del et inc   24

100. Rustic Fountains or "Mete Sudanti" (etching by G.F. Venturini, 1691)

101. Fountain of the Swans (etching by G. Maggi, 1618)

which grew laurel, myrtle, and *corbez-zoli*. In the first decades of the 17th century, with the labyrinths already gone, the two big squares were subdivided into four *parterres* and in the following decades these would be enriched with elaborate *broderies* in the French style. Two squares were decorated like the original *parterres* of water delimited by a rocky rim. In the center, two **Rustic Fountains** (n. **28**) rose. Today these still exist, even if the pools were reconstructed using different shapes around 1930.

The two fountains, rustic versions of the never constructed Metae Sudantes at the center of the Fish Ponds, were made up of a pyramidal structure in big blocks of Tiburtine tartar. From the summit of these structures a jet of water shot out and fell back over the rocks, collecting in pools buried into the ground.

Though they appear identical, in part because of the mineral deposits which have distorted their shapes, in reality they are different in form. The one on the right is a massive rock reef with four niches in the base. The one on the left is in the form of a four-fronted arch reinforced in the center with a pylon. This last fountain is among the most likely sources of inspiration for Bernini's *scogliera* in the Fountain of the Rivers in Piazza Navona, which was explicitly described by contemporaries as a new "Meta Sudante." In the background we

see the **Fountain of the Swans** (n. **29**) at the center of a terrace-belvedere. The little display of water realized in the first years of the 17th century is in a state of notable decay and has lost its sculptural ornamentation as well as the original decoration in stucco and mosaic. In the original configuration, which in part reused Roman statues taken from the Grotto of Venus on the level of the Oval Fountain, there is a Venus in white marble, embedded on its left flank with her loose hair and some sheets of poppies in her hand. It was placed in the central niche. On the sides are two putti seated on geese, a boy embracing a swan on the top of the frontispiece and more swans, dolphins and vases.

The iconological theme of the Sleeping Nymph was usually linked in renaissance fountains to complex, meaningful symbols. In this 17th century composition, it is reinterpreted in an idyllic key. Of all the statues – sold in the late 17th century – their fates are unknown, except for one of the putti – now in the Vatican.

The little terrace beside the fountain, like all the lanes that run along the edges of the garden on the south west, is a favored view point overlooking the valley, with the Sanctuary of Hercules Victorious in the foreground on the extreme right, beyond that the Porta Ro-

Fontana in cima al Giardino di Tiuoli

102. Fountain of the Swans (watercolor by E. Roesler Franz)

mana, below the circular complex of the Temple delle Tosse, and in the distance the bend on the Tiber. The road that curves as it descends is the via degli Orti, the old entrance route to Tivoli which follows the path of the *Clivus Tiburtinus*.

The road was improved by order of Ippolito and it is marked by his usual interests: on one side was the canal which collected the waters discharged from Villa d'Este and were now used for irrigation; and also to delimit the layout. On the other were the high walls of the agricultural lands which here one entered through wide gates.

The various levels of the hillside were extensively cultivated up to the Este Gardens, beneath the villa. Here were vineyards planted with *pizzutello* grapes, derived from *cornichon* grapes imported from France by Ippolito. They eventually became one of the most famous agricultural products in the region, but are now disappearing.

Climbing up the via degli Orti one has the best overall view of the garden, with the imposing foundations which support the terraces well visible, and above this the citadel created by Ippolito, rising, superimposed above the medieval historic center of the town.

Beside the open space in front of the fish ponds we stop to admire one of the most enchanting views of the garden, not by chance reproduced in books, post-cards and brochures as the symbolic image of Villa d'Este.

At the base of the viburnum hedges on the right of the piazza, some partially completed travertine pieces are arrayed. These are from the group called **Neptune on his Cart pulled by Four Sea Horses** and it was intended to be installed in the never completed Fountain of the Sea. This was to be a semi-circle opening to the Tiburtine panorama through a succession of arcades.

The construction of this water theater would have required the demolition of the **Tower of Barbarossa** (n. **30**) one piece of the medieval city wall which was instead conserved, encasing it in the foundations of the terracing and afterwards reopened with an arcade towards the countryside.

We walk now along a section of the avenue on the right side of the Fish Ponds and then turn right towards the ramp which climbs the slope.

According to the 16th century plan, the three stairs which climb from the Fish Ponds towards the Avenue of the Dragons and then to the Avenue of the Hundred Fountains was meant to be flanked by parapets and *gradone* from which unusual water plays would be activated, but only the **Stairs of the Bollori** (n. **31**) ever came to fruition. Begun in 1565 by the stone cutter Rafaello Sangallo and completed in 1570, it was considered by the fountain maker Curzio Donati to be

103. Stairway of
the Bollori
(watercolor by
E. Roesler
Franz)

"the most beautiful aquatic scene in all the villa."

The lower part, which follows the most gradual incline of the first slope, is a paved ramp with travertine borders. On the section between the Avenue of the Dragons and the Hundred Fountains, where the incline reaches around 20%, it becomes a steep stairway divided into two ramps, with fifty-four travertine steps.

Despite the non uniform steepness and the differing conformations of the steps, the stairway is treated in uniform style and flanked on both sides by twenty-one squared pilasters in travertine which hold up an equal number of little basins, among which are arranged eighteen tiny rectangular pools, Thanks to an ingenious hydraulic system, the water flowed from one basin to the next through the

mouths of masks sculpted on one side of the pilasters and reappeared in the next basin higher up, generating the effect of the "bollore," or boiling.

For some time now (and until the next restoration) the little fountains have not been in operation due to damage caused by cypress roots planted in the 17th century. These trees were planted to accentuate the longitudinal axis of the installation.

Therefore the visitor can not really appreciate how, using a modest hydraulic flow, the 17th century technicians were able to create an effect of great volume of water which provided a murmuring accompaniment to the visitor making his way up the tiring ascent of the slope. It is likely that the idea of using water as an ornament of a staircase derived from ancient examples of Hispano-Arabic gardens described by Andrea Navagero in a letter published in 1556. In any event, the water stairs at Villa d'Este were the first in a series of ever more spectacular creations which followed in the 16th century and after.

At the end of the ramp, without climbing up the stairs, we turn right via the Avenue of the Dragons, the background of which is made up of the **Fountain of the Owl** (n. **32**) built by Giovanni Del Duca between 1565 and 1569. This makes up – including the Fountain of Proserpina and the Rometta – a spectacular sequence of rising nymphaeums placed on the artificial terraces which make up the south west zone of the garden. The complex of the three fountains, linked by stairs, constitutes an extraordinary "architectural landscape" in contrast with the walkways through vegetation in the rest of the garden.

Inside the wide rectangular court – open on three sides and articulated by a succession of arcades and niches with stucco tubs – the tall triumphal elevation of the fountain stands apart. It is entirely decorated with polychrome marble tiles. In the center, the great niche is framed by ionic columns covered with tartar, as are the lateral counter-pilasters: in this way the decorative tilework of the columns stands out even more sharply. These feature the twisting shoots of the apples of the Hesperides.

On the roof top the coat of arms of Ippolito is raised up by two angels and flanked by two feminine figures: the display culminates with the Este eagle with two lilies in counterpoint.

Inside the niche, over a tartar *scogliera* one can still see (if not completely) the decorative installation molded in stucco by Ulisse Macciolini in 1568. In the original layout, two youths held a goatskin from which ushered forth a stream of water which poured into an alcoved *baccelato* tub held up by three satyrs. The group, believed lost, was rediscovered during the restorations of 2001-2002 under a large mass of mineral deposits and earth accumulated in the lime-rich waters of the Aniene. The architectural features of the piece remained in fair condition while the more fragile figures of the youths and satyrs were reduced to ruin or are completely gone.

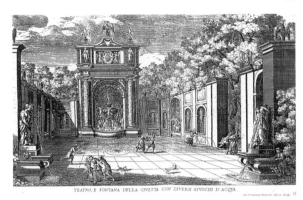

TEATRO, E FONTANA DELLA CIVETTA CON DIVERSI GIVOCHI D'ACQVA

By 1566, the scenic installations were functional in the musical invention created by the French fountain maker Luc Leclerc, thus dating this before the Fountain of the Organ.

The visual component was quite elaborate. In the niche, twenty painted bronze birds were placed on two metal olive branches. These sang – each with their own music. At the appearance of an owl

104. Fountain of the Owl (etching by G.F. Venturini, 1691)

105. Enclosure of the Fountain of the Owl

106. Detail of
the large niche
of the Fountain
of the Owl

107. Elevation of
the Fountain of
the Owl

they grew still. Then, when the owl went away, gradually the music started up again. Finally they all sang together. It is believed that their singing was so life-like and appropriate to each species that it actually attracted the real birds of the garden.

Thus, one might imagine the delight of Cardinal Ippolito's guests during the convivial gatherings in the area, delighted by the music of the waters and the song of the birds, both real and fake.

This musical automaton, inspired by an ancient invention of Erone di Alessandria (sec. 1), was the first to be recreated in the modern era that perfected the technique. Much admired by people of the period, it became a model for many European gardens. It functioned at least until the end of the 17th century, even if it required continuous repairs and replacement of the metal parts which were degraded by the constant action of the water.

The extreme fragility of the decorative materials in mosaic, crushed stone, stucco, and plaster also required innumerable restorations: indeed, even in 1572, when Leonardo Sormani was hired to place eight *peperino* satyrs (now lost) in the niches, already the fountain was ruined and in need of salvage.

At the end of the 19th century, after a long period of abandonment, the wall coverings were now completed ruined. They were almost completely reconstructed in 1930 under the guidance of Attilio Rossi and again restored in 2001 and 2002.

During the recent work, the large niche was the scene of a sensational discovery: beyond the decorative elements, under a large mass of calcified deposits, some pieces of the original pneumo-hydraulic system were recovered. These included the wind chamber, pieces of abduction tubes for both air and water, and parts of the gear mechanism which moved the owl. This discovery permitted Leonardo Lombardi to plan the reconstruction of the apparatus in conformity with the 16th century model. The work has now been executed by Rodney Brisboe at Diss, in Great Britain.

The birdsong is produced by a mechanism analogous to that used in the hydraulic organ: a jet of violently whirling water enters a vertical tube that extends into the wind chamber. The whirlpools capture air that is then released in the wind chamber and sent to a series of small pipes which are partially immersed in water to prevent the air from being released continuously, thus producing an intermittent series of chirps that resembles birdsong.

A hydraulic wheel causes a toothed cylinder to rotate, opening the valves according to a programmed sequence, thus causing the organ pipes of varying sizes (and tonalities) to emit their sounds.

One portion of the cylinder is left without teeth: as this section passes, the birdsong ceases while the owl appears. The movements of the predator are controlled by a device involving a bucket which fills with water and then lowers, causing the rotation of a reel linked to an axle which is anchored to the owl. When the bucket reaches the end of its track, a valve opens which causes it to empty and a counterweight takes it back to the top. This, in turn, causes the reel to rotate in the opposite direction and thus, the owl goes away. The birds progressively begin to sing again and the cycle starts over. Technical linkages guarantee synchrony.

To partly hide the mechanism and also to replace an image to go with the sound of the birds, a work by the master Emilio Farina has been recreated in the niche. This is a reinterpretation of the original decoration, done in painted profiles.

Climbing a few steps on the left of the nymphaeum we find the front of the **Fountain of Proserpina** (n. **33**), named also "of the Emperors" because it was intended to contain the statues of four Roman Emperors who had construct-

ed villas in the Tiburtine: Caesar, Augustus, Trajan, and Hadrian.

The squared enclosure conceived as an open-air circle was realized by Alberto Galvani in 1569-70 and closed on two sides by stairs which lead to the Rometta (the one on the left is not useable because the steps of the last ramp no longer exist). Along the parapets there are water chains with shells and masks. The walls beneath are covered with vestments in tartar flakes framed by bands of marble tiles.

The back wall is structured as a triumphal arch, with three spans marked by twisting columns of a composite order, inspired by the columns of the Vatican basilica, the provenance of which medieval tradition linked to the Temple of Solomon. These are the so-called

108. Fountain of Proserpina or of the "Emperors"

"salamonic" columns used also in the pictorial decoration of the Salon on the lower floor of the palace.

The lateral spans are articulated by niches with stucco shells in the basins and frames with scenes in bas-relief, mostly lost. The central arch is framed in a smoothed rustication which breaks the frieze of the trabeation, which is decorated with acanthus volutes alternating with 'grotesques." The grotto continues in the depth of the foundations with a polylobed structure covered with tartar pieces in the form of stalactites. The central niches house a stucco sculptural group, *Pluto kidnapping Proserpina*, placed here around 1640. Only Pluto remains, on his shell being borne by two sea horses. In the side niches two tritons riding dolphins are represented sounding the *buccina*.

This fountain, too, has been restored many times, both in its hydraulic system and in its decoration. Already in 1607 there was a first intervention by Orazio Olivieri and the most recent was done in 1987.

Climbing the stairs to the right one reaches the **Fountain of "Rometta"** (n. **34**). This is positioned at the end of the symbolic course of the waters captured from the Tiburtine mountains (represented by the Oval Fountain) which run quickly towards the valley and unite in the Tiber at the gates of Rome.

The fountain, planned by Pirro Ligorio and realized by Curzio Maccarone between 1567 and 1570, presents a view of ancient Rome.

According to an anecdote reported by Audebert (1576) Cardinal Ippolito wanted to include in his garden the model of Rome because Pope Pio V had blocked him from building a grand and superb palace – the size of a castle – in the city. As a result, he decided to build it in Tivoli, affirming that if he couldn't have permission to have a castle in Rome, he would have Rome (or at least Rometta) in his castle.

The water theater is placed on a wide, semi-circular terrace, supported by imposing pilasters linked by a double order of arcades and extending out towards the valley well past the line of the medieval wall which had marked the south-west edge of the garden. In the first decades of the 19th century, the structures underwent notable decay which caused the demolition of the architectural background in 1850, except for a limited portion of the model on the left.

The effect of the volumetric composition and the design in its entirety are documented in the engravings of Ven-

109. Rometta (etching by G.F. Venturini, 1691)

110. on the following pages: Water displays in the Fountain of Rometta

111. Statue of
Rome Victorious

turini (1691). On a high podium – like a theater stage – a hemi-cycle opened onto the miniature version of ancient Roma, linked visually with the real city, visible in the distance.

The ensemble of little buildings was divided into seven parts, corresponding to the seven hills with their most important monuments, linked by gates which represented the gates of the city. There were arches and aqueducts, and each of the seven hills, according to the *Descrittione*, "had on it something that made it recognizable – a temple on top – the most famous, made by the ancient peoples such as for example on Mount Palatino there is the Temple of Apollo, which was very famous among the ancients, and each temple has its own statue made of marble, by which it was easy to recognize which temple it was."

The urban prospect was reproduced from Trastevere and crossed to the center, the Capitoline Hill, following the point of view of the maps of ancient Rome drawn by Pirro Ligorio between 1552 and 1561.

At the center of the scene, on axis with the Tiburtine Sibyl on the opposite side, arises the statue of *Rome Victorious*, sculpted in 1568 by the Fleming Pierre de la Motte, on a design by Pirro Ligorio. In front we see the *She Wolf*

Nursing the Twins, executed by the same artist but placed here only in 1611.

Below the podium, the Tiber can be seen, represented by the marble statue of the river in the grotto on the left, which, as the *Descrittione* reports: "copied the real Tiber moving and irrigating the bases of the hills, and running around almost all of Rome." The waters then calm, widening in a low pool, around the boat with an obelisk as a mast, symbol image of the Tiburina Island, dedicated in ancient times to Aesculpius, God of medicine.

At the beginning of the 17th century, on the left slope of the urban landscape, an artificial mountain was molded. This was shot through with cascades and streams, reproducing the morphology of the rock spur of the Tiburtines with its waterfalls and cascades, thus reaffirming the "background" of the principle scene, that is to say the links between Rome and the territory of Tivoli, from whence derives its life-producing waters.

On the summit of this formation there is a stucco statue of the river God Aniene – who holds in his right hand the circular Temple of the Sybil. Below, half-hidden in a grotto, there is the figure of the Appenines who holds in his arms the mountain from which is born the river whose water – after tumbling down the cascades – merges into the Tiber.

The naturalistic scene was completed by a group of statues in peperino arranged on the lawn below the waterfall: animals, goatherds, farmers, and shepherds (one actually in the act of relieving himself) introducing a note of farce into the sacredness of the theatrical 16th century scene. These were removed at the end of the 17th century.

Climbing from the piazzale on a short flight of stairs, we reach the **Fountain of Flora** (n. **35**) which marks the start of the diagonal path rising to the palace. Located in linkage with the Fountain of Pomona at the other end of the Hun-

112. "The Tiburtine Mountain" and the statues of *The Aniene* and *the Appenine* seen from the Rometta

dred Fountains, it has a similar structure but a different decorative scheme. This too was cleaned around 1930; the mosaic vestments of the arcaded prospect presents the motif of the Apples of the Hesperides and the molded elements placed on the crown of the cornice are made up of Este eagles flanked by lilies.

The restoration of 2002 which reintegrated and consolidated the wall coverings and the decoration allowed also the possibility of bringing back to light the original stucco and shell ornamentation of the back wall, which had lain hidden under thick layers of mineral deposits. Left of the fountain, a ramp continues into the shadows of the laurel and viburnum wood. Do note the majestic ancient ilex with an extraordinary scaffolding of branches.

Arriving at the little square where several paths meet, we can take a short rest before the final climb, taking the level avenue to the right that leads to the little loggia above the Fountain of

Flora, with a pretty view towards the Rometta.

Turning back, do not neglect to observe on the right the root structure of the ancient grizzled ilex on the retaining wall of the embankment which gives a good idea of the difficult marriage between the vegetation and the artificial terraces on which the garden is built.

Climbing the last ramp to the right of the little square, we return to the Cardinal's Walk, at the end of which we find the **Grotto of Diana** (n. **36**), with which we conclude the route of the visit. The grotto is visible only from the outside due to the extreme fragility of its constituent materials.

Dedicated to the hunting goddess and virgin, and therefore "to honest pleasure and chastity," as indicates the *Descrittione*, the "chamber nymphaeum" in a cross-shape exploits the vaulted supports of the upper terraces.

The grotto maintains a large part of its glittering decorative coverings, which involve all the surfaces and include multiple ornamental motifs composed of many materials, such as stucco bas-relief, tiny colored and enameled mosaics, paste vitree of crushed rock, sea shells, and glazed majolica. Some materials which rendered it even more precious disappeared long ago, such as the gemstones that adorned the eyes of the bas-relief figures "lifted," according to Zappi, in 1576, "by some evil-doers and mad men," or the corral branches which enriched the central niche. The decoration was executed in 1570-72 by the Bolognese Paolo Calandrino who imprinted his name in the scrolls on the pedestals of the four caryatids on the

113. on the previous page: Grotto of Diana (in the background, the bas-relief with *Diana and the nymphs on the hunt*)

114. Grotto of Diana (in the foreground, the bas-relief panel with *Diana transformed into a tree*)

sides of the principal fountain, of which only fragments remain.

From the entrance, one continues to a rectangular vestibule covered by a crossed vault. On the lateral walls two niches open which contained statues: on one side the *Pentesilean Amazon* and on the other another *Amazon* (or, *Lucrezia*), surrounded by mosaics with plant motifs, masks, armor, and Amazonian pelts. The strata of the vaults, divided by bands with branches of the apples of the Hesperides weaving in spirals, are decorated with cornucopia, floral motifs, and lilies. Four oval frames contain reliefs in polychrome stucco: *Perseus saving Andromeda from the Sea Monster, Andromeda thanks Perseus, Europa kidnapped by Jupiter transformed into a Bull* (of the fourth scene almost nothing remains).

The central recess is delimeted in the angles by caryatids (one is missing) which support baskets of fruit on their heads. From these, shoots of apples spring out, weaving and crossing with

115. *Perseus liberates Andromeda* (detail of the vault of the Grotto of Diana)

116. Mosaic decoration of the vault of the Grotto of Diana

the decorations of the vault, culminating at the center with the white Este eagle. On the vault are marine scenes with Tritons and Nereids appearing with grotesque motifs.

A large semi-circular niche opens on the rear wall. Here there is the rustic fountain which originally harbored an ancient statue of Diana. Behind the tartar *scogliera*, a backing of leafy trees and rocks appears in high relief of stucco. This is sheltered in a seascape: the burning sun with its long rays light up the sea on which a sailing ship travels towards a coastal town.

The central recess is arrayed in two rectangular spaces under barrel vaults: in the one on the left, thre is a rustic fountain which contained a statue of Minerva with provenance traced to Villa Adriana, though the plans had dictated instead a statue of the chaste Ippolito, with clear reference being made to the name of the Cardinal. On the right, a loggia facing the Tiburtine landscape is decorated with mythological scenes and mosaic grotesques. The walls of the lateral recess are adorned with great bas-relief panels which are now badly deteriorated. These depict *Minerva and Neptune, Minerva and the Muses, Diana and the Nymphs on the Hunt,* and *Daphne transformed into a Laurel.*

The back of the nymphaeum conserves a wide section of the 16th century majolica flooring, from the original composition in tiles of various formats arranged around hexagons, created by the master Bernardino de' Gentili di Aversa, in 1572.

Lilies, eagles and apples, heraldic emblems of Ippolito constitute the recurrent motif alternating with a myriad of figurations: cottages, *fraticelli*, dragon heads, cupids on dolphins, fish, hares, pheasants, wolves, geese, pelicans, and other animals are placed with floral motifs or geometrical designs, with profiles of people and portraits of gentlewomen, some with writing beside them, such as

117. Detail of the 16th century flooring in polychrome majolica from the Fountain of Diana

118. Statue of an *Amazon* (Capitoline Museums, Rome)

"Laurentia," or "Portia," or "Cornelia;" in others only the names "Amore," "Fede-Orte," "Roma," "Nabuli," "Cremona," and the date "1572."

This fountain, too, has lost its original sculptural array. All the statues were acquired by Benedetto XIV in 1753 for the Capitoline Museums, where they remain today.

BIBLIOGRAPHY

ABBREVIATIONS

AMSTSA
"Atti e Memorie della Società Tiburtina di Storia ed Arte"

Ashby T., *The Villa d'Este at Tivoli and the Collection of Classical Sculptures*, in "Archeologia" 1908, pp. 219-256
Azzi Visentini M., *La villa in Italia. Quattrocento e Cinquecento*, Milano 1995

Barbieri P., *Organi e automi musicali idraulici di Villa d'Este a Tivoli*, in "L'Organo" 1990, pp. 3-61
Barisi I., *Tivoli, Villa d'Este*, in Cazzato V., Fagiolo M., Giusti M.A. (a cura di), *Atlante delle grotte e dei ninfei in Italia*, 2 volumi con saggio introduttivo di M. Fagiolo, Milano 2001-2002
Barisi I., Fagiolo M., Madonna M.L., *Villa d'Este*, Roma 2003
Belli Barsali I., Branchetti M.G., *Ville della Campagna Romana*, Milano 1975
Bernini D. (a cura di), *Memorie artistiche di Tivoli*, Roma 1987

Coffin D.R, *The Villa d'Este at Tivoli*, Princeton 1960
Coffin D.R., *The Villa in the Life of Renaissance Rome*, Princeton 1979

Del Re A., *Dell'antichità tiburtine, libro V*, Roma 1611
Dernie D., *The Villa d'Este at Tivoli*, London 1996
Desnoyers G., *La Villa d'Este à Tivoli ou le songe d'Hippolyte. Un rêve d'immortalité heliaque*, Paris 2002

Fagiolo M., *Natura e artificio: l'ordine rustico, le fontane e gli automi nella cultura del manierismo europeo*, Roma 1979 (1981)
Fagiolo M., *Il significato dell'acqua e la dialettica del giardino*, in *Il giardino storico italiano*, atti del Convegno (Siena 1978), Firenze 1981, pp. 197-210
Fagiolo M. (con M.L. Madonna), *Roma delle delizie. I teatri dell'acqua: grotte, ninfei, fontane*, Milano 1990
Foglietta U., *Tyburtinum Hippoliti Estii (MDCIX)*, con traduz. di F. Sciarretta, Tivoli 2003

Imparato I., *Relazione del Bernini sulle fontane e sulla Villa d'Este a Tivoli*, in "Archivio storico dell'Arte" 1890, p. 132-138

Lamb C., *Die Villa d'Este in Tivoli*, München 1966
Lazzaro C., *The Italian Renaissance Garden*, London 1990
Lightbown R.W., *Nicolas Audebert and the Villa d'Este*, in "Journal of the Warburg and Courtauld Institutes" 1964, pp. 165-190
Lutz H., *Kardinal Ippolito II. d'Este (1509-1572)*, in *Reformata reformanda. Festgabe für Hubert Jedin*, Münster 1965, pp. 508-530; traduz. ital. in AMSTSA 1966, pp. 127-156

Madonna M.L., *Il Genius Loci di Villa d'Este. Miti e misteri nel sistema di Pirro Ligorio*, in M. Fagiolo, *Natura e artificio*, Roma 1981, pp. 190-227
Madonna M.L., *La "Rometta" di Pirro Ligorio in Villa d'Este a Tivoli: un incunabolo tridimensionale*, in M. Fagiolo, *Roma antica*, Lecce 1991
Monssen L.H., *An enigma: Matteo da Siena Painter and cosmographer? Some considerations on his artistic identità and his fresco landscape all'antica in Rome*, in "Acta ad archaelogiam et artium historiam pertinentia", 1989, pp. 208-313
Monssen L.H., *Nature, Virtue and Sacrifice: a reading of the Room of the Fountain in the Villa d'Este at Tivoli*, in "Acta ad archaeologiam et artium historiam pertinentia", 1989, pp. 131-208
Montaigne de M., *Journal de voyage en Italie (1580-81)*, traduz. ital., Firenze 1958, pp. 39-46

Pacifici V., *Ippolito d'Este, Cardinale di Ferrara*, Tivoli 1920 (rist. Tivoli 1984)
Pacifici V., *Villa d'Este*, in "AMSTSA" 1921, pp. 58-90
Pacifici V., *Luigi d'Este. Capitolo VIII: Villa d'Este*, in AMSTSA 1937, pp. 154-80, 1938-39, pp. 173-78, 1940-41, pp. 125-156

Rossi A., *La Villa d'Este a Tivoli*, Milano 1935

Schwager K., *Rez.* a D.R. Coffin 1960, in "Kunstchronik" 1962, pp. 7-20
Seni F.S., *La Villa d'Este in Tivoli*, Roma 1902

Tosini P., *Girolamo Muziano e la nascita del paesaggio alla veneta nella villa d'Este di Tivoli*, in "Rivista dell'Istituto Nazionale d'archeologia e storia dell'arte", 54, 1999, pp. 189-231

Zappi G.M., *Annali e memorie di Tivoli*, a cura di V. Pacifici, Tivoli 1920

INDEX

De Luca Editori d'Arte

Editing
Federica Piantoni

Technical coordinator
Mario Ara

© 2004 De Luca Editori d'Arte s.r.l.
Via E.Q. Visconti, 11 - 00193 Roma
tel. 06-32650712   fax 06-32650715
e-mail: libreria@delucaeditori.com
ISBN 88-8016-613-1

Printed June 2004
by Tipar s.r.l. - Rome